THE C2C CYCLE ROUTE

About the Author

Jeremy Evans has produced books on all of his favourite outdoor activities, with titles covering sailing, windsurfing, trekking, camping, power-kiting and inline skating, as well as cycling on road and trail. In the early days of mountain biking, Jeremy pioneered 300 cycle routes across the UK, then discovered the delights of riding Audax marathons up to 400km. When family life intervened, Jeremy encouraged his wife and three daughters to enjoy extensive cycling tours in France, Switzerland and the UK. Needless to say, his family all helped to ride and research the magnificent C2C route, cycling across England's finest landscape from coast to coast.

THE C2C CYCLE ROUTE

by Jeremy Evans

2 POLICE SQUARE, MILNTHORPE, CUMBRIA LA7 7PY
www.cicerone.co.uk

© Jeremy Evans 2011
First edition 2011
ISBN: 978 1 85284 649 7
Reprinted 2014 (with updates)

Printed by KHL Printing, Singapore
A catalogue record for this book is available from the British Library.
All photographs are by the author unless otherwise stated.

Advice to Readers

While every effort is made by our authors to ensure the accuracy of guide-
books as they go to print, changes can occur during the lifetime of an edition. If we know of any, there will be an Updates tab on this book's page
on the Cicerone website (www.cicerone.co.uk), so please check before
planning your trip. We also advise that you check information about such
things as transport, accommodation and shops locally. Even rights of way
can be altered over time. We are always grateful for information about
any discrepancies between a guidebook and the facts on the ground, sent
by email to info@cicerone.co.uk or by post to Cicerone, 2 Police Square,
Milnthorpe LA7 7PY, United Kingdom.

Front cover: Looking west, a superb downhill from Whinlatter Pass to High Lorton
with wonderful views towards the Irish Sea and Solway Firth

CONTENTS

Route symbols on OS map extracts

route

alternative route

linking route

start point

finish point

alternative start point

route direction

bike shop, café

food shop, pub

For OS symbols key see OS maps.

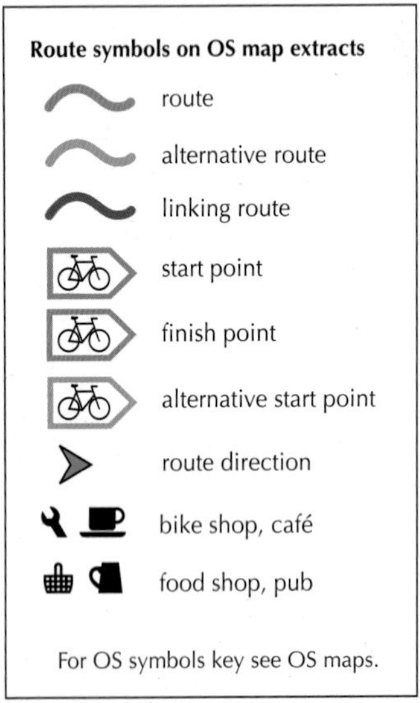

Some parts of the C2C are best suited to mountain bikes, but when the going is really rough there are always suitable road options (Stage 4, looking west)

SUSTRANS AND THE C2C

On 11 September 1995 UK Charity Sustrans received £43.5 million from the National Lottery to create the National Cycle Network (NCN), a series of traffic-free paths and quiet on-road routes that connect to every major town and city and pass within 2 miles of 75 per cent of the population, stretching 14,000 miles across the length and breadth of the British Isles. In 2012, over three million people made 485 million journeys on the National Cycle Network, which was extended by 500 miles. Based on average car emissions, the potential carbon dioxide saving of Network journeys was around 884,000 tonnes. Trips made by children on the National Cycle Network numbered 81.4 million, including an estimated 18.4 million to and from school. Sustrans' maintenance responsibilities along much of the Network cost £1 million during 2012, and as a charity they are reliant on donations and funding to be able to keep these much-loved routes in great shape.

Riding through Lorton Vale on the edge of the Lakeland fells

'Terris Novalis' is among the most impressive sculptures on the C2C route

The NCN was created and developed by Sustrans as part of its work to promote walking and cycling, both for local everyday journeys, and for longer-distance leisure rides. From the 17-mile Bristol and Bath Railway Path where it all began, to the latest new flagship route – the 170-mile *Way of the Roses* through Lancashire and Yorkshire – the Network scales mountains, crosses divides, races through cities and takes leisurely ambles through the countryside.

The Sea-to-Sea (C2C) route is perhaps the best known and most iconic of all Sustrans routes, and when you look through the pages of this book, it's easy to see why. It was originally created by Sustrans as the first long-distance cycle route in the country, as well as the first fully coast-to-coast route. It came about after Sustrans built local routes at either end of the ride, and then decided to develop a route linking them together, using substantial sections of traffic-free paths, It is now the UK's most popular 'challenge' cycle route, passing through the northern Lake District before climbing the Pennines, 'the roof of England', and then descending to the railway paths of County Durham.

Whether on-road or traffic-free, the NCN has grown to become an integral part of the UK's transport network and carrying over one million journeys every day, it has exceeded all expectations. There are now more miles of Network than there are of motorways with over 50,000 signs, 10,000 seats and thousands of bridges, viaducts and tunnels along its fascinating routes.

So whether it's for business or pleasure, commuting or just for fun, travelling on the network has something for everyone as well as being a fundamental part of how people in the UK get around everyday.

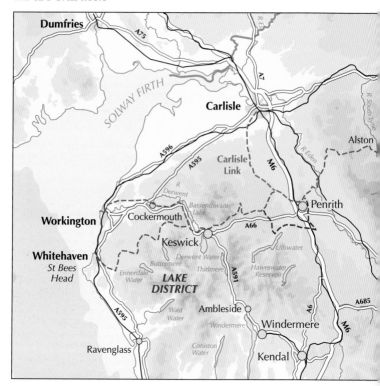

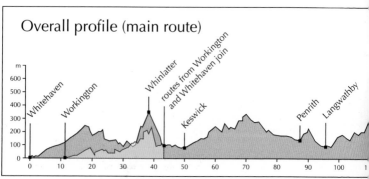

Overall profile (main route)

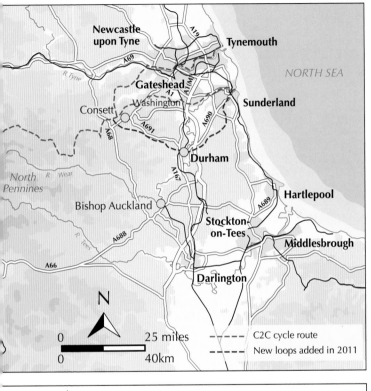

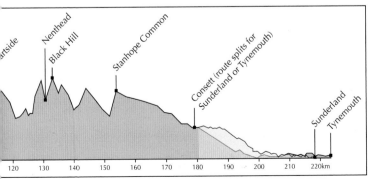

The start of the off-road route across Stanhope Common, just opposite the Rookhope Inn (Stage 4)

INTRODUCTION

Downhill past Grove Rake Mine along Redburn Edge – the finest downhill section on the west–east C2C (Stage 4)

Do you like beautiful scenery, excercise and plenty of fresh air? Are you interested in Britain's remarkable industrial heritage? Do you enjoy visiting village pubs and cafés? Are you up for cycling up and down a few hills? If the answer is yes, you will love riding the C2C.

The Coast to Coast (C2C) is a superb 219km (136 mile) cycle route across northern England that connects the country's Irish Sea and North Sea coasts. It passes through the Lake District and Pennines, home to some of Britain's most dramatic landscapes. In addition to endless wonderful views across the countryside, the C2C offers a great selection of interesting places to visit. The route is accessible and enjoyable for bike riders from novice to expert, including children of most ages. It is equally enjoyable as a leisurely tour for recreational riders or as a full-energy ride for those who enjoy 'cycle sportif'.

The C2C first opened as a formal route in 1994. It is a cyclist's version of Alfred Wainwright's famous Coast to Coast Walk, but follows a shorter route with considerably fewer hills. The route was designed by Sustrans (see pages 8–9) and is now Britain's most popular long-distance cycle route. Thousands of cyclists complete the C2C each year, but there is plenty of space and it never feels crowded.

Great care has been taken to make the C2C as cycle-friendly as possible. Approximately half the route follows dedicated cycle paths or off-road tracks that are traffic-free. Most of the other half follows quiet roads that are particularly well suited to cycling. There are a few short sections on busier roads in built-up areas, but these are relatively stress-free.

In this guide the route is described over five days – an ideal pace for leisure cyclists and families that allows time for detours to look at places of interest along the way. (Shorter itineraries are also included for those who enjoy a challenge.) The detailed route information, accompanied by OS maps, is suitable for cyclists of all levels, and the guide offers lots of help with planning and undertaking your C2C adventure.

WHY DO IT?

The route can easily be completed in five days by those with a basic level of fitness. If you cycle further and faster, it's possible to ride from sea to sea in four, three or two days – and, for the super-fit, even in one day. Riding the route is an excellent way to get trim and healthy – you will feel in great shape by the end of it.

Most of the C2C route follows traffic-free cycle tracks or quiet minor roads, allowing you to enjoy cycling with minimum stress or danger from

The final traffic-free part of Stage 1, with the outskirts of Keswick directly ahead

traffic. Excellent signposting makes the route easy to follow with straight-forward route planning using a conventional map or GPS.

There is plenty of accommodation along the way, which makes planning an itinerary easier, as well as a very good choice of places to eat and drink. In addition, there are bag-carrying services operating along the route and companies offering package trips, including accommodation (see 'Specialist C2C companies', below).

The C2C is a great challenge. You will feel justly proud of the achievement of cycling from sea to sea!

CHOOSING YOUR ROUTE

The route in this guide is described from west to east, as this is often held to be the 'best' direction in which to cycle the C2C – however, the choice is yours (see 'West to east or east to west?', below, and a summary of the east–west route in Appendix D).

The C2C has two different start and finish points at both ends of the route – a choice between Whitehaven or Workington on the west coast and Tynemouth or Sunderland on the east coast.

Cyclists riding the C2C for the first time would be advised to start from Whitehaven (or nearby St Bees) and finish at Tynemouth. However, consider starting from Workington if you'd prefer less hill-climbing on the way to Keswick, and finishing at Sunderland (if you don't mind missing Newcastle)

if you'd prefer to avoid the somewhat tortuous final section to Tynemouth.

West coast
On the west coast, the routes from Whitehaven or Workington to Keswick are very different.

Whitehaven is the most popular start point for the C2C, leading directly to the Lake District, where it passes between Loweswater, Crummock Water, Bassenthwaite Lake and Derwent Water. There are two significant climbs to Kirkland and Whinlatter, but the reward is great downhill riding and wonderful views. But Whitehaven is not a perfect place to start. The route out of the town is well signposted, but probably the most unattractive part of the whole C2C.

St Bees provides an interesting link route to the C2C. This is the start of Wainwright's sea-to-sea walking route. The place is much smaller and quieter than Whitehaven, just a few miles to the south – one stop away on the train with a good connecting route provided by Hadrian's Cycleway (NCN Route 72). St Bees is a pleasant place to stay overnight before starting the C2C cycle route, which gives cyclists the opportunity to walk up to St Bees Head and dip their feet (or front tyre) in the Irish Sea. Starting at St Bees is recommended for those who don't mind missing the official start of the route.

Workington, to the north, provides a very different route to Keswick via Cockermouth, staying north of

Viaduct on the outskirts of Cockermouth, on the way from Workington to Keswick (Stage 1b)

the Lake District until it approaches Bassenthwaite Lake. It's less spectacular than the Whitehaven–Keswick route, mostly because there are fewer big hills. Cockermouth is an interesting small town to visit or stay at en route to Keswick, and the final section towards Bassenthwaite Lake is particularly good for those who enjoy off-road trails. Major floods during November 2009 caused extensive damage in Workington and Cockermouth, but Sustrans and the local authorities have done an excellent job keeping the C2C route open for cyclists.

Maryport, 9.5km (6 miles) along the coast to the north of Workington, provides an interesting option for an overnight stay for those who start (or finish) the C2C at Workington. It's a

smaller and more attractive town than Workington, with fine views across the Solway Firth. Hadrian's Cycleway provides a link route to Workington, or there is a direct connection by train.

East coast

On the east coast cyclists also have a choice of finish (or start) routes in either Sunderland or Tynemouth (the route divides at Consett).

The route to **Sunderland** is slightly shorter and potentially a little faster than riding to Tynemouth. At least 90 per cent of the distance is traffic-free, following cycle paths and disused railway tracks. Most of the route is pleasant enough, but unremarkable, until the final few miles alongside the River Wear, which provides a superb finish to the C2C. The nearest rail link is Sunderland central station, connecting with the C2C via a signposted cycle lane.

The route to **Tynemouth** is a little longer, but more interesting. It's virtually all traffic-free and very enjoyable riding between Consett and Newcastle, where the riverside waterfront is extremely attractive on a fine day. Cyclists might expect to complete the C2C with a pleasant ride along the River Tyne from Newcastle to Tynemouth, but the river is seldom seen at all. Instead the route gets fiddly and can be a little frustrating, particularly with diversions caused by roadworks, which should improve over time. The last part of the route, cycling round the marina and harbour towards the finish, is suitably fine. The Metro railway has a station within easy reach of the Tynemouth start/finish of the C2C, but it refuses to carry bikes (unless they are 'folders'), which is a major let-down at the end of Britain's premier cycle route. Instead, cyclists have either to ride back to Newcastle, where the main railway station is not particularly easy to find, or to take a taxi (the standard 'black cab' will take two bikes and riders).

Alternative routes between Keswick and Sunderland

One of the delights of the C2C is that throughout its length there is a choice of routes. In addition to the alternative start and finish points, there are some interesting variations on the central section from Keswick to Consett.

Stage 2

- Some 9.5km (6 miles) west of Keswick, the C2C turns north towards Beckside and Mungrisdale on the eastern

The cycle path on the Tynemouth option follows the River Derwent through to the River Tyne (in the background) (Stage 5b)

side of the Lakeland fells, after which the main route turns south to follow the side of the busy A66 trunk road. The alternative route follows quiet roads north-east and south-east from Mungrisdale.

- A new optional southern loop is routed via Ullswater, Askham and Lowther Estate, rejoining the main C2C to the east of Penrith.

Stage 3

- At Four End Lane, 9.5km (6 miles) from Langwathby, an off-road route leads due west to Selah Bridge and is recommended for mountain bikers. Road bikers are better off on the longer road route via Renwick, which is very pleasant.

- At Selah Bridge, the road route climbs up to meet the A686, from where there is a steady climb to Hartside Café at 580m. Grinding uphill while being overtaken by cars and lorries is not much fun, and in dry, fine weather a better alternative is to use the off-road track that leads uphill from Selah Bridge. It gets steep and requires a long push, but affords magnificent views.

- Alston is several kilometres off the C2C route and well worth a visit. It is signposted as Route 68 at Leadgate and follows the River South Tyne valley to the centre of the old town.

- Between Garrigill and Nenthead there is the option of riding on- or off-road. Both routes involve a

Looking westwards from the bottom of the off-road track above Selah Bridge – take time to stop and enjoy the superb views (Stage 3)

Start of the track that leads up towards the final high point at Bolts Law (Stage 4)

long climb. The road route is very quiet and pleasant, as long as it doesn't involve riding into a head wind. The off-road route is almost twice the distance, with some parts steep and rough, but it is recommended for keen mountain bikers who have plenty of time.

Stage 4

- At Nenthead an alternative off-road route leads directly to the top of Black Hill – the highest point of the C2C. It's shorter than the road route, not too steep or rough, and a very good choice for those who prefer to avoid traffic and tarmac.
- At Rookhope there are two routes to Parkhead. The road route is slightly longer and goes via Stanhope, which is an interesting village. The main drawback

is that it ends with just over 3km (2 miles) of riding quite steeply uphill on the B6278, which may be busier than cyclists would wish with traffic. The off-road route crosses grouse moors run by the Stanhope Syndicate. It is a superb ride with magnificent views, but the route is closed occasionally during the grouse-shooting season (12 Aug to 10 Dec). This is indicated by signs at either end but the closure dates are not publicised in advance.

Taster Route 4

- The Old Coach Road provides a superb off-road route leading eastwards from Castlerigg Stone Circle near Keswick, which links via minor roads to the main C2C route at Greystoke (Stage 2).

Some of the Old Road is steep and rough. It provides a far more dramatic view of the Lake District than the road route, but will probably take twice the time.

Stage 5a
• A new optional route connects Consett to Sunderland in a southern loop via the cathedral city of Durham.

West to east or east to west?

West to east is generally regarded as the best direction to cycle the C2C for two reasons. First, the prevailing winds blow from the west, and, secondly, the hills are longer when approached from the east, and shorter (but also steeper) when approached from the west.

However, it is conditions on the day that really count. West to east is perfect if there are steady westerlies pushing from behind, but not so great if there is a strong easterly while crossing the Pennines, where cyclists can be very exposed to a hard grind against the wind. The truth is that strong winds are not much fun from any direction. Light winds are a cyclist's best friend.

As to the hills, some are hard and long, but give a wonderful downhill ride in the opposite direction. Some hills are short and sharp, which makes them too steep for a really good downhill in the opposite direction. Again, the most important consideration is likely to be the prevailing weather, with contrary winds (and rain) transforming a steady hill climb into a struggle.

Nevertheless, there's little doubt that the majority ride from west to east. This is worth considering for those who are riding the C2C on a busy weekend. Meeting large groups of cyclists on narrow tracks and lanes can be a bit unnerving, particularly if they are hammering downhill on blind bends. It's probably safer to go with the flow.

A summary of the route from east to west appears in Appendix D.

WHEN TO GO

The simple answer is, 'When the weather is perfect'. That means blue skies to make the most of wonderful views, no rain, very light wind blowing in the direction you are cycling, and the temperature neither too hot or too cold (around 20–25°C should be near perfect for cycling).

The problem is that the Lake District is notoriously wet, and the high hills of the Pennines are very exposed to poor weather at all times of year. Cyclists have been forced to abandon the C2C due to extreme wind and rain during August, but they were very unlucky. November through to March is best left for experts seeking a winter challenge. Ice and snow are common hazards at this time of year, roads on the high hills may be closed, off-road sections may be waterlogged and very muddy, and short days leave little room for delays.

April through to October can be a wonderful time to ride the C2C, but beware that spring or autumn can also

Perfect weather and superb cycling country as this C2C rider heads towards Allenheads (Stage 4)

provide gale-force winds and unseasonably low temperatures for the time of year. Summer is the best time but good weather can never be guaranteed.

It makes sense to check the weather outlook on the web. BBC Weather (http://news.bbc.co.uk/weather) provides five-day forecasts, updated every few hours, for principal towns along the route, including Whitehaven, Workington, Keswick, Penrith, Alston, Consett, Newcastle, Sunderland and Tynemouth. But unless the forecast is truly terrible – gales and non-stop rain – you should go ahead and enjoy the ride. It's surprising how much of the C2C route is relatively well protected at low levels, particularly on some of the disused railway

lines. It's also surprising how quickly the rain can clear up and go away.

Do be aware, however, that summer is peak holiday season. The Lake District will be particularly busy, making it advisable to book hotels, B&Bs and camp sites well in advance. Away from tourist-traps such as Keswick, cycling the C2C is remarkably quiet.

GETTING THERE AND GETTING BACK

Train stations

The rail network does not do a great job of covering the C2C (much of the route is quite off the beaten track), but the following key places along the way have a rail link.

- Carlisle links with Workington and Whitehaven on the west coast (but avoid rush-hour trains which are likely to be full)
- Penrith and Langwathby both link with Carlisle, which has a link route (Route 7) with the C2C.
- Newcastle Upon Tyne provides a high-speed link with London and the south, as well as a cross-country route to Carlisle.
- Chester-le-Street (east of Newcastle) is within 1.5km (1 mile) of the C2C between Stanley and Washington, but has no dedicated cycle link.
- Sunderland has a cycle link to the C2C and is within 3km (2 miles) of the start/finish, via Newcastle Upon Tyne.

For more information contact www.nationalrail.co.uk.

Taking bicycles by train

For cyclists planning to travel by train, it is vital to check that bikes can be taken on board, as some train companies have restrictions on this, especially at busy times. (On www.nationalrail.co.uk, go to the Train Companies page, select the train company you are travelling with and look at the Onboard Facilities section.) Where accompanied cycles are carried there is no charge. A comprehensive leaflet, 'National rail cycling by train' can be downloaded at www.nationalrail.co.uk.

National Rail has the following advice for cyclists travelling by train.

- If a cycle reservation is required make it as far in advance as possible.
- Cycles are not carried during periods of restriction.
- Label your cycle clearly.
- Cover your folded cycle.
- Tandems, tricycles and bicycle trailers are not carried unless otherwise stated.
- Unaccompanied cycles cannot be carried on any services.
- Cycles must be carried in the designated area on trains and must not obstruct doors or aisles.
- Cycles are carried at owner's risk.

Getting home

It is important to plan what happens when you reach the end of the C2C. There are five likely options

- ask someone to collect you from the finish
- pre-book a train ticket for you and your bike
- pre-book a minibus/baggage-transport service to return you to the start and collect your car

Motorised support team picks up the bikes at Nenthead, an interesting place to visit (Stage 3)

- arrange to have your car delivered to the finish
- ride your bike back to collect your car from the start.

The train is relaxing after such a long ride and environmentally friendly, but for those with time, the last of these options is also highly recommended. The C2C links directly to the 300km (187 mile) **Reivers Route** (NCN Route 10) from Tynemouth to Whitehaven and into the 280km (174 mile) **Hadrian's Wall Cycleway** (NCN Route 72) from Tynemouth to Ravenglass on the west coast, passing through Workington and Whitehaven. Cyclists who have reached the end of the C2C should be fit enough to take on either of these interesting routes. The Reivers provides a more hilly challenge through remote border country, while the Hadrian's Wall route follows the famous Roman wall and forts of the Cumbria coast.

Other link routes

In addition to the Reivers Route and Hadrian's Wall Cycleway, the C2C links to three other National Cycle Network routes.

- **Three Rivers** – 264km (164 miles) connecting Middlesborough, Stockton, Hartlepool, Durham, Consett, Newcastle and South Shields
- **Coast & Castles South** – 355km (221 miles) connecting Newcastle to Edinburgh via Berwick and Melrose

The Penrith to Carlisle route also links with the Reivers Route (NCN10), both on-road and off-road ('Taster routes', Ride 5)

- **Lochs & Glens South** – 425km (264 miles) connecting Glasgow to Carlisle (C2C link to Penrith) via Dumfries and Glenn Trool

PLANNING YOUR ITINERARY

Some people like to cycle the C2C in a day. A popular target for hot-riders is to complete the almost 225km (140 mile) route in under 12hrs, which requires an average speed close to 12mph. That may not sound fast, particularly compared to travelling by car, but anyone reading Dylan Noble's report in 'Planning your itinerary', below, will appreciate the very serious challenge that a non-stop C2C represents.

Stretching the C2C over several days makes the riding a lot easier, and the main part of this guide describes a five-day itinerary, aimed at leisure cyclists. Although overall cost increases with each night's accommodation, the advantage is that extra time allows more enjoyment of all that the route has to offer.

Plan carefully and set a sensible target for each day. Do not be over optimistic. It's better to arrive too early than too late. Allow for delays due to bad weather and give yourself plenty of time to explore the most interesting places along the route, which are likely to include Cockermouth, Keswick, Alston, Beamish Museum and Newcastle.

A hard rider may be able to average 12–15mph on the C2C, but cyclists taking it easy, enjoying the views, stopping for snacks and riding on some of the alternative off-road sections are likely to have an average speed of 7mph or less. It sounds slow, but is not when you consider that the C2C is above all a dramatic route. And what's the hurry? You are there to enjoy it.

Five days
- Excellent timescale for leisure cyclists and families who like to take it easy, and a great choice for those who feel a little unsure about being able to complete the route.

- Average distance of about 48km (30 miles) a day, allowing time to enjoy each stop-over or postpone cycling due to rain.
- Four nights' accommodation required, with the option of one or two extra nights if staying at one or both ends of the route.

In the five-stage route described in this guide, the fourth stage ends at Consett for ease of description because this is the point where the route splits before continuing to either Sunderland or Tynemouth. However, in practice, a good place to stay on the fourth night is The Old Station at Parkhead,

Parkhead Station serves food, provides accommodation and welcomes cyclists in a delightful isolated location at the west end of the Waskerley Way (Stage 4)

25

about 8km (5 miles) short of Consett. It's a pleasant place, and you can rest in the knowledge that your final day is all downhill. Cyclists taking this option may also choose to stop earlier on the third night, at the lively Pennine village of Alston, rather than at Nenthead, 8km (5 miles) further on.

Four days

- Sensible timescale for regular cyclists and people with a good level of fitness who want to enjoy all the route has to offer.
- Average distance of about 64km (40 miles) a day – quite a bit more demanding than the five-day itinerary.
- Minimum of three nights' accommodation, plus extra nights at either end.

Three days

- Good choice for sporty, fit cyclists who enjoy a challenge.
- Approximate average distance of 80km (50 miles) a day is demanding, with less time to enjoy stopovers; cyclists likely to feel pretty tired at the end of each day.
- Minimum of two nights' accommodation plus extra nights at either end.

Two days

- Only recommended for serious hard riders who enjoy a major challenge.
- Average of more than 112km (70 miles) a day is very demanding,

with little time to enjoy the attractions of the C2C. Except for very keen mountain bikers, cyclists will have to restrict themselves to riding fast on tarmac and miss out the optional off-road sections.
- Minimum of one night's accommodation, for some serious rest, plus extra nights at either end.

One day

- Very high level of fitness and preparation required. This is purely a challenge ride.
- No time to enjoy the views or any delights that the C2C has to offer slower cyclists.
- But you'll save on accommodation!
- No itinerary is required – you ain't stopping…

See Appendix B for some suggested 4, 3 and 2-day itineraries.

C2C day rides

Anyone living or staying near the route can ride the C2C as separate day trips. This has two advantages – cyclists can pick when and how far to ride, according to the weather, and may save a lot of money on accommodation.

This works well for cyclists with a support team, willing to drop and collect by car. Alternatively, circular and linking rides (see 'Taster routes') make it possible to enjoy part of the C2C and then return by bike or train.

THE C2C IN A DAY

In Whitehaven harbour: a wet start to a long day

Dylan Noble, a nutritionist and personal trainer, and Neil Robinson decided to ride the C2C in one day in 2010. Dylan tells the story of one hard day...

We planned to set off from the coast of Whitehaven, about an hour from my home near Penrith, at 7.30am on Friday 16 July. But, inevitably, last-minute preparations and alterations to provisions delayed our start to about 8.30am. Howling wind and heavy rain didn't inspire much confidence, and Whitehaven harbour, where we suited up for riding, was unsheltered from the rain. So we didn't hang around!

We struggled to find the cycle track that leads out of Whitehaven initially, but were soon impressed by the C2C cycle-path network on old railway tracks, where knocking off the miles seemed easy. Occasionally, these C2C paths turned into off-road sections on rocky tracks that would have been excellent and enjoyable on a mountain bike, but were a nightmare on road bikes, as we wanted to take all precautions to avoid punctures.

As we progressed through the journey, the weather improved steadily, which was fully welcome, since the start of the ride is still up there amongst 'My top ten worst miles on a bike'. Cycling straight into a strong, wet breeze

27

was not a nice way to start the day. But like any negative in life, it helped to challenge our commitment and made us appreciate good times to follow. And these we certainly had – on the best country roads the Lake District has to offer, cycling towards our destination with a brisk westerly tail wind to help us all the way. Great riding!

Highs and lows

The first major milestone was getting up and over Hartside. Once we arrived at this point, I think we made a rookie mistake and took a slightly over-extended stay, filling bottles and stocking up on flapjacks. After an approximate 15min pit stop the weather was once again not pleasant at all. We were both stone cold and pretty much soaked through. To make matters worse I'd forgotten to pump up my tyre, so we had to stop shortly after and fix that, with me thinking, 'This is the coldest I've ever been on a bike.' It definitely was the only occasion when I wished I was riding uphill instead of downhill! But our grumpy mood soon brightened, when we arrived at the base of the valley and were greeted by a first appearance of the sun, which was, well… indescribable!

There were further low points along the way, particularly since we repeatedly lost the route, but most notably when I raced off down a hill trying to reach maximum speed, only to be told at the bottom that we had missed a right turn at the very top! The climb back up wasn't too much fun, but I have to commend Neil, who continued chasing me, even though he realised we were off-route less than halfway down that hill. Probably the lowest point that both of us distinctly remember was the seemingly never-ending climb out of Stanhope. I thought I could see the peak three times, only to discover a higher peak beyond.

Fortunately, the best point followed quickly after we reached the summit of this monster and could finally set eyes upon the finish line, with a clear view of the distant North Sea and eastern coastline dazzling in the late afternoon sun. All the pains and strains vanished, and we both continued riding with a surprisingly fresh pair of legs, only to suffer pain once again 5 miles later when the excitement wore off and a puncture set in. The final approach towards, and ride through, Sunderland seemed to take an age. But we finally arrived at the location we'd been dreaming of for the previous six weeks, in spite of almost being beheaded by youths casting fishing lines across the route just a few metres from the finish.

The end of the day

Having started pedalling at approximately 8.30am in the morning, we eventually stopped at around 8.45pm in the evening. Our time was just over the 12hr mark. I was a little disappointed to come so close, but without the misfortune of a puncture late in the ride and better knowledge of the route, I am confident we would have been able to break the 12hr barrier. Maybe next time. Overall, I would recommend a road bike if you want to ride the C2C as a challenge and complete the ride in good time. My next project is to ride the off-road coast-to-coast route on a mountain bike. Much rougher terrain will stretch the difficulty and probably make it a two-day trip, but it should still be fun!

SPECIALIST C2C COMPANIES

Bag carriers

There is no need to carry lots of gear on your bike, as there are several specialist companies that will collect a cyclists' bag each morning and deliver it to their next hotel, B&B or camp site by the time they arrive in the late afternoon. In addition, these companies can provide parking and return transport for yourself and bike at the end of the C2C in order to retrieve a car, or provide transport for anyone unable to ride a section due to illness or exhaustion. Prices are reasonable. For instance, the Sherpa Van Project charges £39 per bag (two minimum), or £79 (2013 prices) for baggage and return transport on a five- or seven-day C2C. (See Appendix C for some recommended companies.)

Organised C2C trips

A number of companies offer a complete C2C package, with itineraries of varying length, which includes accommodation and bag and bike transfers. The basic package includes pre-booked accommodation, with options of packed lunches, luggage transport, return transport and extra nights' accommodation. They provide clear directions and large-scale maps, and can organise off-road parking for the duration of the trip, helping to make the C2C experience as stress-free and enjoyable as possible. C2C Hassle Free offers a different style of package based on staying three or four nights at Mains Farm Camp Site, almost halfway along the route where the Pennines get steep, with daily minibus transport to and from each section. (See Appendix C for recommended companies.)

WHERE TO STAY

For those cycling the route independently, it is advisable to book accommodation in advance for each night. There is a very good choice of B&Bs,

hotels and camp sites, as well as pubs, cafés and restaurants all the way along the route.

Although some flexibility is lost by pre-booking, be aware that accommodation may be booked solid, and there is nothing more depressing than being turned away time after time. (It sounds like a great idea to stop riding when you're tired, when it starts raining or when you simply like the look of a place, but it is not wise to rely on places being available.) Remember that the Lake District is a major tourist area. There are a lot of places to stay and a lot of people who want to stay in them. Further afield, there is less demand and consequently less accommodation available, making things just as difficult if you turn up at the door. Apart from that, it really helps to have a schedule and a target to keep you focussed on the day's ride.

The internet has made it much easier to find accommodation (see Appendix C).

Camping

Pitching your tent in a camp site provides the cheapest accommodation on the C2C, but camping does have its disadvantages. Carrying a tent, sleeping bag and cooking gear adds a lot of weight and bulk to your bike. Putting up a tent is a hassle after a

A food stop at the cycle-friendly Lakeland Pedlar (Stages 1a and 1b)

hard day on the saddle, particularly when the ground is sodden and it's pouring with rain.

There is a limited choice of camp sites along the C2C route, which will dictate where and when you stop. It is vital to book ahead in the summer season. Wild camping is not permitted or possible.

CHOOSING YOUR BIKE

The C2C route is almost evenly split between minor roads and traffic-free paths, tracks and cycleways. All the roads have well-maintained tarmac surfaces, suitable for full-on road-racing bikes. Surfaces on traffic-free sections may be tarmac, cinder, stones or even mud in wet weather. Some of the going is quite bumpy and rough, becoming extremely rough on some of the alternative off-road sections. The result is that the choice of bike involves a compromise.

- **Lightweight road racer** These have lightweight frame, drop handlebars and skinny 23 or 25mm tyres. They are very fast on well-surfaced tarmac roads, but uncomfortable and bumpy on all but the smoothest traffic-free paths, with potential for punctures or the nightmare of a buckled front wheel. Many road racers have double chain rings, which require more physical effort to ride uphill than the triple chain rings fitted to most mountain,

touring and hybrid bikes. The bikes are no good for carrying an overnight bag, and would have to be carried on rough tracks. If there is rain, expect to get very wet and messy without mudguards.

- **Mountain bike** A lot of people appear to choose mountain bikes for the C2C, but maybe that's simply because they only own a mountain bike. Nevertheless, these are a reasonably good choice, and perfect for riding on rougher surfaces – particularly super-rough tracks like the Old Coach Road out of Keswick, which will provide lots of fun on a full-suspension mountain bike. They are much slower than the road racer on smooth tarmac, due to greater weight and rolling resistance, with wide, knobbly tyres and smaller 26in wheels. For cyclists who choose to keep off the roughest tracks, it may be worth buying a set of smooth road tyres for a faster ride. A mountain bike should be easy to pedal uphill, with lots of gears, and easy to control downhill, thanks to a sit-back position with straight handlebars. It's advisable to fit a mudguard over the front and rear wheels. Fitting a pannier rack to a mountain bike can be tricky, reducing the amount of gear you can carry. A single-wheel mountain-bike trailer would solve that problem, but pulling one wouldn't be much fun on the C2C.

- **Touring bike** This is a classic style of bike for long-distance touring. It looks similar to a road-racing bike with drop handlebars, which help to vary your riding position, but is heavier and more durable, with slightly wider wheels and tougher tyres, full-length mudguards, pannier racks for luggage and a great gear range for easy pedalling uphill. These bikes are a good compromise choice for all surfaced roads and many traffic-free paths on the C2C, although it may be a bumpy ride without suspension. Tyres are much narrower than a mountain bike, so they will have to be pushed on rougher tracks, which could be tiresome with a heavily laden bike.

- **Audax bike** These are a specialist cross-over between a touring bike and lightweight road racer, fitted with mudguards and lights, and slightly more heavy duty than a racer, with wider gear ratios. Audax bikes are used for long-distance cycling events over 100, 200, 400 or even 1200km. They are a good choice for those who want to complete a fast C2C and spend as much time as possible on roads.

- **City bike** A sit-up bike designed for pedalling around town and watching where you go is not a great choice for the C2C, owing to the extremely undynamic riding position for tackling hills, but it is still capable of getting from coast to coast.

- **Hybrid** This cross-over between a touring, city and mountain bike, with lots of different permutations, is probably the best compromise solution for the C2C.

Recommended features

- **Riding position** that gives the option of sitting up to enjoy the view or dynamic riding up and down hills.
- Medium width 700x35mm **tyres**, such as Schwalbe Marathon Plus, to combine easy rolling with excellent grip, durability and puncture resistance, plus reasonable handling on rougher tracks. Wider diameter tyres give a softer, more forgiving ride on paths and tracks.
- Lightest possible **frame** and components, making it reasonably easy to push the bike and ride up hills.
- Front **suspension** is useful to soak up the bumps on a hybrid or touring bike, but not if it adds a lot of weight. Functional, lightweight suspension comes at a premium price.
- Very good **brakes**. Either V-brakes with wire cables or hydraulic disc brakes. The latter are most

efficient, but can interfere with fitting racks and mudguards, as well as being considerably more difficult for DIY maintenance.

- A wide range of derailleur **gears**, with triple chain rings at the front and eight or nine cogs at the back, will tackle any hill on the C2C with ease.

- A good set of full **mudguards** is vital for riding through mud, puddles and rain. Make sure they are securely fitted, with good clearance, so that mud and crud do not clog up inside.

- A strong, secure rack mounted over the rear wheel is extremely useful, so that gear can be carried in two **panniers** with space for a rack bag on the top. Front panniers allow even more gear to be carried, at the cost of making the bike more cumbersome to handle and very heavy to pedal or push uphill.

- Horizontal, flat **handlebars**, which may be a little swept back, help provide a dynamic riding position. 'Riser' handlebars, with the ends lifting upwards, make it possible to sit up and enjoy the view. It's just a matter of finding

A bike with back panniers and a front rack bag outside the Cyclists' Barn, Greystoke (Stage 2)

the right compromise for your kind of riding. Comfortable grips are important. If they feel hard, wear a pair of cycling gloves with padded palms, which also take the shock out of a bumpy ride. 90° bar ends can be useful for changing riding position.

- Riding 225km (140 miles) makes it important to have a reasonably comfortable **saddle**. They range from squidgy gel saddles that promise to be soft on your backside to hard leather – the choice is yours. Remember that for maximum pedalling power and comfort the saddle must be at the correct height, with the down-stroke leg almost (but not totally) straight at the bottom of the circle.

- To achieve maximum pedalling power, use clipless **pedals**. However, a pair of simple 'bear trap' pedals suits this kind of ride very well, enabling cyclists to wear trainers or sandals and still storm up those hills.

- Fitting the bike with **lights** is sensible, even for cyclists riding the C2C in mid-summer. You may get delayed and still be riding as dusk falls or get caught by thick mist on the high hills. In either case, it is important to be visible on murky roads. Except for cyclists who expect to ride in the dark, flashing LEDs provide an ultra-bright, low cost, lightweight solution.

- A handlebar-mounted cycle '**computer**' is optional, since the C2C map provides a very effective 'mile counter'. It's useful to be able to record your mileage, and it may be interesting to log average or maximum speed, but a significant disadvantage of using a computer is that it's easy to get transfixed by those little numbers clicking off the miles, when you should be enjoying the views.

Bike hire

What if you don't have a suitable bike or are flying in from overseas? No problem – you can hire one. For instance, Haven Cycles provides a dedicated hire service from premises in Whitehaven within 500m of the start of the C2C. A choice of alloy hybrid or mountain bikes is available for adults or children, fitted with mudguards, rear racks and a basic toolkit. Prices (in 2013) are £45 for up to three days then £5 per day thereafter. The company can also provide secure parking, baggage transfers, en-route cycle repairs and recovery service, cycle collection and transport back from the finish, and a minibus service with cycle trailer for Newcastle or Manchester airports.

Pedal Power offers a C2C bike-hire and baggage-transfer service from Amble in Northumberland, Ainfield Cycles of Cumbria offers a cycle-hire service that allows cyclists to collect a bike at the start and leave it at the finish of the C2C, and Darke Cycles provides cycle hire at the eastern end of the C2C in Sunderland. See Appendix C for contact details.

THE C2C ON FOLDING BIKES

Si Trickett and Steve Brindle, both aged 34, commute to work on Brompton folding bicycles with two-speed gears designed for city cycling. For a change of scenery, they decided to unfold their bikes and ride the C2C...

The Brompton is a unique British-manufactured bicycle, mainly used by commuters in combination with trains. Many cyclists consider them to be some sort of a joke bicycle, suitable only for slow riding on very short journeys. In fact, in spite of their small wheels Bromptons have a long wheelbase coupled with rear suspension to give a good ride. They can be used by the tall to the very small, have a range of gearing options from single to a wide-range six speed, and are fitted with an excellent luggage system. They also fold small, so fitting them into cars and onto trains is a doddle, including services where cycles are not permitted (such as the Metro at the end of the C2C in Tynemouth). We both have the Brompton S2L configuration designed for city commuting on fairly level roads, with flat handlebars and two gears – one for getting away from the lights and climbing fairly easy hills and one for zipping along the flat. The ratios are not entirely suited to powering up steep hills in Cumbria and the Pennines!

When we told people our plan to do the C2C on our two-speed Bromptons, we heard many a story about evil hills to climb along the route. It has to be said there were some very long and very steep climbs, sometimes both steep and long. We would also be first to admit that we needed lower gears, but still managed to grind up all the C2C climbs and carry our luggage with a decent amount of zig-zagging – with the exception of the very steep 200m stretch coming up out of Garrigill. Zig-zagging on this bit meant that we were just going back and forth across the road and not getting anywhere, so we got off and pushed! However, we both got a great sense of achievement from grinding past a group of mountain-bike riders, who were pushing their bikes uphill in spite of their low gears, having earlier taken the mickey out of us for doing the C2C 'on giant kids' bikes'. It's not what bike you have, it's what you do with it! Our next challenge is doing the Land's End to John O'Groats route on the Bromptons, aiming to take eight days to complete the 1000 miles!

THE C2C ON UNICYCLES

A group of eight riders rode the C2C in August 2010, but cycling on two wheels wasn't enough of a challenge. Peter Haworth outlines the challenge of unicycling the route and shares some tips...

An average 35 miles per day might not sound a big deal to many two-wheeled cyclists, but unicyclists generally ride a lot slower, with pedals driving the single wheel directly at a low 1:1 ratio. My comfortable cruising speed on the flat is around 9 or 10mph, so taking the fairly hilly terrain of the C2C route into account, this meant at least 5hrs in the saddle every day, with no chance of freewheeling, even on downhills. But, thanks to an amazing support team and a lot of perseverance, we did it, overtaking two-wheeled cyclists on the steep climbs but struggling (and, very occasionally, getting down) on the downhills, and raised a few thousand pounds for the British Heart Foundation on the way.

Tips for one-wheeled success

The best thing you can do to prepare is to check your equipment before you set out. Carrying sufficient spares and having the skills to use them was vital to our success, but a bit more preventive maintenance in the weeks before the ride would have made things go a lot more smoothly.

Training is also crucial, especially if you don't normally ride long distance. As well as getting yourself into shape, you'll get an idea of the suitability of your equipment for the challenge. Most weeks, I ride less than 30 miles. By the summer I was commuting at least 15 miles every weekday, with an extra 30–40 mile ride each weekend. In the five months leading up to the actual event, I clocked up over 1700 miles, which is quite a lot more than I'd normally ride in a whole year, and I'm sure I wouldn't have lasted much past the first day of the C2C without those miles under my belt.

Finally, the biggest revelation I had was about lubrication. Spending hours in the saddle without protecting yourself from chafing is just foolhardy, so I'm very glad I was introduced to chamois cream at the start!

You can read all about our adventure at www.pmh1wheel.org and donate to the British Heart Foundation at www.justgiving.com.

THE C2C ON A PENNY FARTHING

On 27 Sept 2007 Dave Preece mounted his penny farthing in Whitehaven harbour. After three days of pedalling and pushing, he reached Tynemouth harbour and was able to declare, 'More people have walked on the moon than have done what I have done this weekend.'

It takes a bit of confidence to ride a penny farthing, but anyone who can ride a bike could ride a penny farthing in a straight line. The handlebars turn as you push down each pedal, which makes riding hard work, with both arm and leg muscles working.

The bike has no gears on the 54in fixed wheel. You could ride up huge hills with a modern bike in such a low gear, but not a penny farthing, because the riding position is so poor. You can't get out of the saddle and have to battle with your arms to keep going in a straight line. I'm a fairly fit club cyclist who enjoys riding up hills on a modern road bike, but if a hill is steeper than about 8 per cent and longer than 200m, I push my penny farthing.

And downhill is plain dangerous! Going up, you gradually get slower to the point where you have to get off. Going down, you have to decide right at the top whether you can ride it. If there is any doubt, you must get off. If you get halfway down and the speed of the bike is starting to run away, you are going to go over the handlebars. The brake is not very effective, so you have to control speed with back pressure on the pedals, which makes downhill riding tough. But in the end, most of the C2C downhills were rideable with care.

Some of the C2C cycle paths were difficult. Rough ground is not ideal, although the big front wheel does smooth out the bumps. The first two days (Whitehaven to Stanhope, in my case) were tough, averaging 7.4mph over 91 miles, with a total ascent of 7170ft, frustrated by innumerable gates on cycle paths and a very long push along rough track in Whinlatter Forest. When I walked, it was because I feared I might damage my front wheel – not easily fixed.

I was worried that riding the last section from Newcastle to Tynemouth on a penny farthing might attract unwanted attention from the local lads, but everyone I met along the C2C gave me plenty of space and just wanted to talk about my curious bike.

www.pennyfarthingmadness.blogspot.com

Bike maintenance

If you have a problem with the bike, there is a good choice of bike shops and mechanics along the C2C route. However, it's a lot better to be sure your bike is in excellent working order before you start and to carry a basic tool kit to fix minor problems on the way (see 'What to take', below).

If you pull a bike out of the garage to ride the C2C, it makes sense to pay a bike mechanic to give it a full service. Alternatively, make your own check that everything is working well. (See Appendix F for how to give your bike a full medical.)

WHAT TO TAKE

The more gear you carry, the harder it will be to pedal uphill. This may seem obvious, but it's worth careful consideration when planning how to ride the C2C. You can choose from three levels – superlight, medium weight or heavy weight.

Superlight

Top choice for C2C record breakers or those who feel confident about riding with very little gear.

Suggested superlight kit list

- saddle bag with minimalist tool kit, including pump, puncture-repair kit and spare tube
- water bottles mounted on bike frame or backpack reservoir
- high-energy chew bars for sustenance
- mobile phone, cash and credit cards
- C2C route map or GPS

Medium weight

At this weight cyclists can carry everything required, with the exception of overnight gear.

Suggested medium-weight kit list

- tool kit (see below)
- first aid kit (see below)
- shorts with optional padded insert
- water-resistant shoes or sandals
- breathable base layer
- wind-proof fleece or jacket
- waterproof jacket and trousers
- sunglasses
- helmet
- lightweight cycling gloves
- drink
- snacks
- mobile phone
- cash and credit cards
- sun-barrier lotion
- bike lock
- map
- C2C guide book

Carrying your gear

- One or two **panniers** (40 litre capacity) on a sturdy rear rack will carry a lot of gear, including spare clothes, tool kit, food and drink. If you only carry one pannier, mount it on the outside of the bike (away from the traffic) as an additional safety feature. Ideally, panniers should be totally waterproof with a simple roll-up system for closing the top. Separate internal or external pockets are useful. Mounting and releasing should be secure and simple, and the panniers easy to carry on a short trip to the shops or hotel. Scotchlite reflectors on the panniers provide another useful safety feature. It is important to have a last-in, first-out packing plan, while ensuring that heavy items are low down. Packing related groups of items together in separate stuff-sacks is also handy.

- A **bar bag** mounted on the handlebars is very useful for small items that need to be easily to hand, such as mobile phone, wallet, compact camera, suntan lotion, sweets and chew bars. Again, it should be fully waterproof, including the clear plastic map case (a useful feature) on top of the bag. Mounting and releasing should be secure and simple – some designs have a strap that transforms the bag into a shoulder bag.

Heavy weight

At this weight cyclists are totally self-reliant for the C2C with everything required to ride the route and stay overnight, but the bike will be heavy. Packing requires expertise, not only so that you can find what you want when you want it, but also to ensure that weight distribution provides a well-balanced ride.

Suggested heavy-weight kit list
In addition to all the items in the medium-weight kit list, clothing for overnight hotels or B&Bs and gear for camping can also be included.
- lightweight trousers
- thick fleece jacket for cold evenings
- spare underwear
- three spare base layers
- shoes or sandals
- basic toiletries including toothbrush, toothpaste, soap, deodorant, etc
- tent
- sleeping bag
- sleeping mat
- torch/lamp
- cooker and cooking utensils

Carrying your gear
- Rear rack – trunk bag or tent between the top of panniers
- Rear wheel – two 40 litre panniers
- Front wheel – two 25 litre panniers
- Handlebars – bar bag up to 8.5 litres

Tool kit
The following are essential unless you're feeling extremely lucky
- small hand **pump**
- **puncture repair** kit – patches, sandpaper, glue
- three heavy duty plastic **tyre levers**

- spare **inner tube** – correct size for tyre and wheel.

It would also be worth taking a few other key items along.
- **Chain lubricant** After heavy rain, the bike chain may need to be re-lubed.
- **Allen keys** 4, 5 and 6mm are the most useful sizes. Available as separate allen keys, three-way allen-key tool or as a simple multi-tool with allen keys, Phillips and flat-blade screw drivers. Buy good quality tools, with allen keys that are a precise fit.
- **Chain breaker** Useful if your chain breaks.
- **Phillips and flat-blade screw driver** Best carried as part of a multi-tool.
- **Adjustable spanner** Useful if the bike has loose nuts.
- **Small pliers** Useful to straighten bent links in a broken chain and for problems with cables. Best carried as part of a multi-tool.
- **Multi-tool** The Leatherman- or Gerber-style multi-tool includes pliers, sharp knife and screw drivers, all of which can be useful for bike repairs. One disadvantage is that good quality multi-tools tend to be heavy.
- **Plastic ties** Keep half a dozen in your tool kit for running repairs.
- **Insulating tape** Generally useful – you never know when.
- **Rag, clean cloth, gloves, hand cleaner** – Mending a puncture

or fiddling with the chain is a dirty job. Light gloves can also be useful.

First aid kit

There is a wide range of 'first aid kits for cyclists' in bike shops. Choose one with a good quality waterproof pack and, ideally, the following contents

- 1 roll 25mm sticking plaster
- 2 fleece compresses, 10 x 10cm
- 1 elastic bandage, 60cm x 40mm with 2 clamps
- 1 gauze bandage, 60cm x 40mm
- 1 pressure bandage, 80cm x 100mm
- 12 plasters, 70 x 20mm.

In addition to the contents of a standard first aid kit, it may be advisable to carry

- zinc oxide or 'climbers tape' for securing dressings, protection against blisters and immobilising fingers or toes
- antiseptic cream such as Savlon, to be used in conjunction with antiseptic cleansing wipes
- paracetamol or aspirin.

Carrying a first aid kit like this sounds sensible, but do you know how to use those dressings or what they are for? Anyone who carries a first aid kit would also be advised to do a first aid course. On the internet there are dedicated first aid courses for cyclists, in addition to standard courses (for example, take a look at www.londonfirstaid.com).

Remember that prevention is better than cure. Cycle safely, wear a good helmet that fits well, and wear gloves or track mitts, which will help protect hands in a fall.

Lock it or lose it

Although you would be very unlucky to have a bike stolen on the C2C, cyclists should lock their bike when it is unattended and check their insurance requirements in case of theft. Overnight, the safest solution is to always use a B&B or hotel that can provide a secure lock-up for bikes – there are plenty of these on the C2C. The alternative is to carry a very heavy, expensive D-lock, but even that may not guarantee against losing seat post, lights or wheels. Panniers and bar bags can be locked to the bike, but for peace of mind keep them in sight (for instance, when stopping at a pub or café) or take them with you.

FOOD AND DRINK

There are plenty of shops, cafés and pubs along the route, and choosing where to stop for a drink or something to eat adds to the fun of the C2C – although it's obviously cheaper and less time consuming to take your own food. Anyone cycling at a leisurely pace should start each day with a hearty breakfast – there is a very high standard at all hotels and B&Bs that serve the C2C. Then stop along the route to buy a simple lunch – bread, cheese and tomatoes, followed by

FOOD FOR THOUGHT

Food becomes seriously important if you plan to tackle the C2C as a one- or two-day challenge ride. Nutritionist Dylan Noble (see 'The C2C in a day' on page 27) gives the following advice on preparing for a challenge ride.

Any attempt at carbo-loading on the night before you start is already far too late. You have got to be sorting out your diet for the entire preceding week, eating lots of pasta, malt loaf, rice, oats and similar energy-storage foods.

Be extremely careful and watch exactly what you are eating, as a balance is essential – you've got to avoid an upset stomach. Remember that all electrolytes (body salts) lost are difficult to balance instantly, and you will lose more electrolytes through sweat on the journey. Lack of body salt will result in conditions such as muscle cramps, which will not be easy to ignore for the remaining 100 miles.

In terms of food for the actual day I took peanut butter sandwiches, bananas, malt loaf, biscuits, isotonic drinks and lots of water. I don't mind carrying a backpack, as I seem to drink a lot more than two bottles of water every 2hrs and really like having a big Camelbak.

For advice on putting together a training or nutrition plan for the C2C, contact Dylan by email at dylan@orangebikes.co.uk.

apples or oranges, will suffice. For snacks and treats, take a selection of cereal bars or a small bag of boiled sweets. At the next stop-over, plan to find an excellent dinner!

Drink is very important, particularly when there is a chance of dehydration in warmer weather – letting this get out of control could ruin your C2C. Simple advice is 'drink plenty' – if you are unlucky enough to ride

the C2C in a heatwave (a rare occurrence), you will need to drink several litres each day.

Some riders swear by 'energy' and 'recovery' drinks sold by bike and sport shops, which can be bought in cans, bottles or as a powder additive with lots of claims regarding carbohydrates and electrolytes. Alternatively, tap water is easier to find and a lot less expensive. One problem is that

Rookhope Inn, last stop before the famous C2C crossing of Stanhope Common (Stage 4)

warm water does not taste pleasant on a hot day. To overcome this, the day before you go put 1 litre plastic bottles of tap water in the freezer, leaving enough room for expansion, then pack them in a plastic bag in the bottom of a sturdy pannier. This should provide refreshing, ice-cold water for most of the day. It is possible to carry 2 or 3 litres of water in a pannier without much trouble, in spite of the extra weight. The obvious disadvantage is having to stop, open the pannier and pull out a bottle when you want a drink.

Many cyclists use the conventional solution of frame-mounted cages for bottles, with the big advantage that you can grab the bottle and take a swig while riding. Purpose-designed bottles with drinking spouts provide capacity up to about 750 ml. Cyclists who prefer this option can use two cages for two bottles to get capacity approaching 1.5 litres. Bottles with a flip-up lid are useful for keeping the drinking spout clean in muddy conditions. All bottles need to be washed carefully to ensure that bacteria does not develop inside. Be wary of bottles that claim to keep drinks cold – volume is reduced by the insulation, and performance may be disappointing.

The best solution for high-performance riders on the C2C is a backpack hydration system such as Camelbak. This comprises a 2 or 3 litre bladder carried on the back, with a plastic tube and 'big bite' valve that offers virtual hands-free operation – it allows cyclists to sip little and often to stay fully hydrated while they ride. It is also very useful for leisure cyclists – the backpack is fairly comfortable, drinking is easy and there is some thermal protection, with taste improved by adding an energy drink. In addition, the backpack should have enough space to carry extra gear.

If you have cycling gear, that's fine. Either SPD (clip-in) or 'clipless' pedals, lycra shorts, a tight cycling jersey and waterproof 'drop back' jacket can all be recommended for any high-powered assault on the C2C. But you don't need to wear specialist gear.

Footwear

Remember that as well as pedalling, you may be pushing the bike on rough tracks. Trainers are a good compromise, providing a reasonably rigid sole that sticks to the pedals, good traction for walking and some protection if you fall off the bike. In summer,

open-toed 'all terrain' sandals help maintain cool feet.

Dedicated cycling shoes fitted with cleats provide greater pedalling efficiency by locking your feet onto the pedals. This is expensive as it involves buying a pair of specialist shoes, SPD pedals and cleats. It is also necessary to learn to 'clip in' and 'clip out', which requires a few practice sessions. Cyclists who go for this option should choose mountain-bike shoes with soles that are suitable for walking on tracks.

Bottoms

Depending on the time of year and expected weather conditions, tight lycra shorts with a synthetic chamois pad are probably the top choice, but they are not essential. Mountain-bike baggy shorts can be very

A variety of different clothing styles, footwear and hydration choices among the unicycling C2C-ers at Rookhope

comfortable, hard wearing and look better than lycra off the bike, and there is the option of three-quarter length for cooler weather in either style. Ordinary trekking shorts made of quick-dry material are fine for the C2C, but may get to look grubby and worn after a few days rubbing against the seat. For women, a skirt can be comfortable for cycling. If your backside starts to ache when wearing any of the above, visit a bike shop and buy a well-padded liner to wear underneath.

Full-length trousers are not great for cycling. If you do wear them, make sure there's good ventilation and a lot of free movement around the knees. Even if you don't cycle in trousers, it is a good idea to carry a pair of lightweight, waterproof trekking trousers that can be slipped over the top of shorts, just in case of rain. Getting caught in a rain storm on the Pennines could get very cold and unpleasant without protective gear.

Tops

Doing fairly long distances on the C2C, it's important to be able to regulate temperature to avoid getting too hot, too cold and, most importantly, sweaty. Wear a long- or short-sleeved breathable base layer, with a windproof fleece as a mid-layer for cooler weather, plus a brightly coloured, superlight waterproof jacket for bad weather. Specialist cycling gear covers all of these requirements, but good quality trekking gear will perform well on the C2C. Wear

bright or fluoro colours to help dozy motorists spot you on a bike.

Gloves

Gloves are optional. Short-finger 'track mitts' with padded palms make it easier to grip the handlebars and will certainly be appreciated if you fall on your hands.

Helmets

Helmets are advisable, but finding the right cycle helmet at the right price is not easy. Look for

- a white or bright colour in order to be conspicuous to motorists
- a precise, comfortable fit with the helmet secured firmly to your head
- a light weight, so that the helmet is hardly noticeable on your head
- the best possible ventilation (this is tricky, as wearing a plastic tub is essentially hot – a helmet may have a lot of holes, but it will take a hot ride on the C2C to discover if they are effective).

FITNESS

Although it might seem that the C2C is only for super-fit cyclists, as it goes straight across the Lake District and northern Pennines, that is not the case. However, everyone who undertakes the route would be advised to undertake some training beforehand in order to get the most enjoyment from the ride. If you have any health doubts, get a general health and fitness check before starting.

There is a simple training formula for a long-distance ride. Aim to cycle a cumulative distance of about ten times the total route over a six-month period before the big event. That would mean logging 2250km (1400 miles) as preparation – after that, the C2C will seem like a breeze. Do not leave training until a couple of weeks before starting the C2C. Even if you don't manage six months of training, you need sufficient time to build up stamina and get used to spending time in the saddle.

This kind of preparation is also vital for sorting out problems with your bike and clothing. For instance, you don't want to discover on Day 1 that your saddle is so uncomfortable that you can't spend any more time on it.

NAVIGATION AND WAYMARKING

The C2C follows sections of Sustrans' National Cycle Network (NCN) that spans the UK (see www.sustrans.org.uk for further information). The C2C uses parts of different 'national routes' that link many of the UK's major towns and cities (National Route 71 covers the western area of the C2C; National Route 7 covers the central area and extends to Sunderland (also linking to Carlisle); National Route 14 links Consett to Gatehead and South Shields; National Route 72 provides a route to Tynemouth via Newcastle;

and National Route 68 provides a short diversion to Alston).

The NCN is very well signposted – blue-and-white signs along its length show a bike logo and the national route number in white in a red box, while regional route numbers are in a blue square. Signs may also show a destination and distance. Signposting is extremely clear, and there are C2C signs at every twist and turn of the route.

This guide shows the route highlighted on sections of OS mapping. (Although OS maps are not required for the C2C, they are useful for exploring the surrounding area.) Sustrans produces an excellent *Sea to Sea (C2C) Cycle Route Map*, which is updated every few years to record any route changes. Cyclists may find it useful to take this map with them, as it shows the NCN route numbers.

GPS provides a modern alternative to a paper map. Waypoints for the route can be programmed into a cycle-oriented unit such as the Garmin Edge, which fits on the handlebars, is waterproof and includes speed, trip, time, altitude and many other functions. The advantage is that you don't have to scratch your head and consult the map when there are no signposts. As long as the correct information has been put into the GPS you can just keep riding. A GPS is most useful for completing a one- or two- day C2C challenge, but optional for riding the route at a more leisurely pace, as it is well waymarked.

A selection of Sustrans signage – you'll get used to spotting the little blue stickers...

STAMP COLLECTING

Sustrans provide a stamping card to record your journey on the C2C, which is enclosed in the *Sea to Sea Cycle Route Map*. There are a number of accredited stamping points along the route, mainly in shops and small businesses, and the card has space to collect these stamps.

USING THIS GUIDE

In the guide the route is divided into five stages, each suitable to be undertaken in one day for those who want to cycle at a leisurely pace. Each stage ends at a convenient place for overnight accommodation. Where there is a choice of two alternative C2C routes (at the start and finish) these are numbered as stages 'a' and 'b'. Two 'link routes' on the west coast that join up with the C2C are also described.

At the start of each stage is a box summarising crucial route information – distance, time, ascent/descent and the start point. In the route description key places are shown in **bold** to help with navigation. There

The end in sight: the C2C route follows the promenade round the edge of Tynemouth harbour (Stage 5b)

also is information on places of interest along the route where you may wish to stop and spend some time.

Each stage of the main route is illustrated with OS mapping, which highlights the route and also has symbols showing refreshment stops, shops, cycle repair places, stamping points and so on. The route gradient along each stage is shown on a profile that accompanies the route description.

At the end of the main route, the guide outlines five circular routes based on, or accessible from, sections of the C2C (see 'Taster routes'), all of which are recommended as day rides. These are followed by useful appendixes that include a route summary table, information on

accommodation and how to prepare your bike for the C2C, and suggested itineraries for cycling the C2C in four days or less.

Cycle-path etiquette

When riding on the traffic-free cycle paths and tracks that contribute so much to enjoyment of the C2C, you will meet other people. If it's a pleasant, sunny weekend you can expect to encounter cyclists of all ages, including families with young children, as well as joggers, pram-pushers, walkers and plenty of dogs. Please be courteous and considerate. Take particular care when passing horses, which are easily spooked by bikes. Slow down and give them plenty of space, just as you would if you were in a car. It's also an idea to greet their riders, as the sound of a human voice can reassure a horse. Leave a good impression, which will help ensure that local people are friendly towards the thousands of C2C cyclists who will follow in your tracks.

Never blast past or make people jump out of their skins. If you approach from behind, it is probably best to indicate your presence with the discreet ring of a bell. A simple device will do the job, without being rude or intrusive. If you get no response, try calling out a friendly 'Good morning' followed by a polite 'Excuse me' and 'Thank you'. With that kind of behaviour, everyone will stay happy!

THE ROUTE

C2C start (or finish) at Whitehaven

STAGE 1A

WHITEHAVEN TO KESWICK	
Distance	50km (31 miles)
Time	3–5hrs
Ascent	863m
Descent	786m
Start	Whitehaven harbour, GR182971

This is the most popular of the two alternative starts to the C2C (see Stage 1b for the Workington route), and passes through more dramatic scenery. It begins with a rather dismal first section, but this lasts only for about 5km (3 miles). After that, riding along the railway path cannot fail to be enjoyable, with the route becoming progressively more impressive as it heads for the high hills. Having left the railway path, the route climbs to the first big high of the C2C at Kirkland, with superb views of the fells and a great up-and-down ride to the first of Lakeland's famous lakes at Loweswater. The last part of the ride features an energetic but enjoyable climb through the Whinlatter Pass, after which it's downhill most of the way to Keswick.

The start of the ride is in the southern part of **Whitehaven harbour**, where there is a large pillar with 'C2C' cut out of the steel. There is no information on the route ahead, but the C2C pillar is perfectly located to dip your front wheel into the harbour, where the water just about counts as part of the Irish Sea.

With the C2C pillar behind you, cycle out of the **marina**, bearing right towards the Beacon Visitor Centre. Follow the C2C signposts and turn left to join the road close to the **Argos store**. (At this point, the C2C does not seem particularly cycle-friendly. Those who don't like the idea of sharing Preston Street with traffic can push their bike along the pavement.) Cross straight over at the large roundabout, where the forbidding hill ahead is thankfully not part of the route. Instead, turn left just past the **large blue store**, currently Focus DIY, joining a clearly signposted C2C tarmac cycle path.

After the DIY store, the C2C follows a wriggling route through the suburbs of Whitehaven, which is not a great introduction to the C2C, and past a recreation ground. The route then runs alongside the modern railway in a somewhat zig-zag fashion, crossing under the track three times before it crosses **Meadow Road** and veers off in an easterly direction to join the **old railway line**, with clear country

WHITEHAVEN

Whitehaven marina is pleasantly-situated and cycle friendly

If the weather is fine, it's worth a pedal around the walled harbour to take in the sights before you leave. The harbour area has been modernised for tourists, with minimal hassle from traffic and plenty of benches to watch the world, eat your sandwiches and dream. Whitehaven's wealth was built on trading slaves and rum, as well as shipping and mining, which helped make it England's third largest port. In 1778 Captain John Paul Jones attacked the fleet in Whitehaven harbour during the American War of Independence, the only time that Americans have ever attacked the English on home ground – they were unsuccessful!

A short distance inland, the old centre of Whitehaven is rather handsome, with Georgian terraced houses and the delightful Church of St Nicholas. Having been partly destroyed by fire in 1971, all that remains is a fine tower surrounded by beautiful gardens, with a chapel for prayer and attractive café for your first coffee-break of the route. (Café open Mon–Sat, 10am–3pm, tel: 01946 62572).

More information www.visitcumbria.com

Railway path between Whitehaven and Cleator Moor

ahead. The bad news is that this railway path is all uphill. But it's an easy, steady gradient on an excellent tarmac surface, and you should scarcely notice the climb when blessed by a following westerly wind. (Of course, it's a wonderfully easy ride in the opposite direction.)

You are now on the Whitehaven to Rowrah railway line, which last carried passengers in the 1950s. It leads past disused station platforms overtaken by nature and under fine old railway bridges – admire the stylish cast iron signposts along the way. Be prepared to share the route with runners, walkers, dogs (mostly well behaved), and grannies or small children on bicycles. Slow down and give them space. You may also be forced to share the path with other people's litter, particularly on the

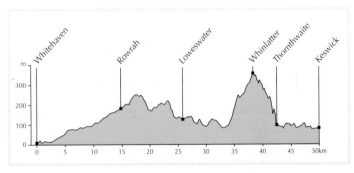

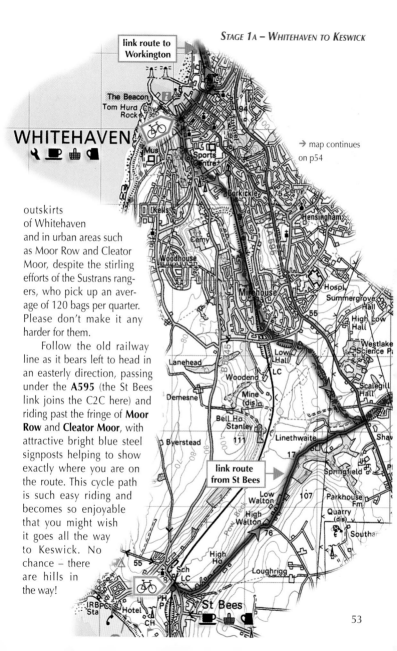

link route to
Workington

WHITEHAVEN

→ map continues
on p54

link route
from St Bees

link route
to Workington

outskirts
of Whitehaven
and in urban areas such
as Moor Row and Cleator
Moor, despite the stirling
efforts of the Sustrans rang-
ers, who pick up an aver-
age of 120 bags per quarter.
Please don't make it any
harder for them.

Follow the old railway
line as it bears left to head in
an easterly direction, passing
under the **A595** (the St Bees
link joins the C2C here) and
riding past the fringe of **Moor
Row** and **Cleator Moor**, with
attractive bright blue steel
signposts helping to show
exactly where you are on
the route. This cycle path
is such easy riding and
becomes so enjoyable
that you might wish
it goes all the way
to Keswick. No
chance – there
are hills in
the way!

About 13km (8 miles) from Whitehaven, the C2C route suddenly leaves the cycle-friendly tarmac path just before **Rowrah** (where you might like to divert to the nearby Stork Hotel if you are in need of a pub), joining an unsurfaced narrow track that winds between old limestone quarries and is part of the **High Leys National Nature Reserve**. The track surface is good, but you can expect to get brown muddy splashes all over your bike in wet weather. After a few enjoyable wiggles, reach the end of this track by a rather fine wooden arch, which is typical of the interesting and unusual decorations scattered along the whole length of the C2C.

Follow the C2C signpost onto a quiet lane, turn right by the school house and enjoy an up-and-down ride through fine open country towards the village of **Kirkland**, which is appropriately situated in the Eden Valley and surrounded by green hills. Pause and look back to appreciate the fine view towards the west coast, then ride on past St Lawrence's Church, which has a fine setting and is well worth a visit for those who enjoy ecclesiastical architecture.

Be prepared for some stiff climbing out of Kirkland as the C2C follows the road below **Keltonfell Top** (295m). The pay-back for all this hard work spinning the pedals (or pushing your bike) is magnificent views across fine country on the fringes of the Lake District. As an added bonus, this road section of the C2C is likely to be extremely quiet, with few cars getting in the way. Ennerdale Water, the westernmost of the lakes, is just over 3km (2 miles)

→ map continues on p56

to the south-east when the C2C turns sharp left at the T-junction by **Cross Rigg**, following the boundary of the Lake District National Park. From here it's all beautiful downhill riding through **Felldyke** towards **Lamplugh**, with a sudden shocking hill climb at the end.

Follow the road as it bears left past Lamplugh Hall, with a chapel on the inside of the bend, then take the next right turn downhill by the

St Lawrence's Church, Kirkland, first high on the C2C

Old Rectory as shown by the C2C signpost. Be prepared for more ups and downs as you ride along the narrow lane towards **Fangs Brow Farm**. The majestic rise of Burnbank Fell hides Loweswater, which is the first lake on the C2C route. Turn right by Fangs Brow Farm, clearly signposted as Route 71, and follow Fangs Brow steadily downhill to **Waterend**, where you get the first clear views of **Loweswater**. This is a very beautiful lake on a fine day, owned by the National Trust and well protected from the horrors of modern development. You could even stay there, as the NT has a small bothy beside the lake, providing very basic self-catering accommodation.

The C2C route follows the road along the north-east side of the lake. If you fancy a picnic (or possibly a swim) it's fairly easy to find an unmarked path running along the water's edge, complete with a few convenient boulders to sit on. If you'd like an alternative leg-stretch, there is a good walking route round the lake, which is 1.5km (1 mile) long. Otherwise, keep riding towards the hamlet of **Loweswater**, where the Kirkstile Inn (www.kirkstile.com) is not only beautifully situated but was also winner of the CAMRA West Cumbria Western Lakes Pub of the Year award in 2009. Anyone riding by in late April might be lucky enough to coincide with the annual Loweswater Beer Festival.

The original C2C route (71) followed the west side of the River Cocker through Lorton Vale with easy riding and gentle hills leading to Lorton Low Bridge. However, the bridge collapsed during floods in November 2009, with the result that the C2C route was diverted to follow the east side of the River Cocker by crossing **Scalehill Bridge** on the direct road out of Loweswater. This is more up and down and longer than

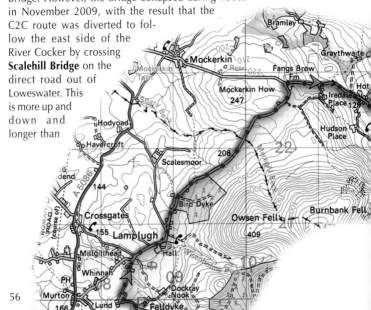

the original route. It joins the **B5289** for a short distance past **Brackenthwaite**, before taking the next right turn (beware of speeding traffic) up a lane that runs parallel to the B5289, while heading north towards High Lorton. This lane is quite hilly and narrow, so watch out for anyone coming in the opposite direction.

Follow the Route 71 signpost and turn right at the next crossroads, cycling past the schoolhouse and small village shop at **High Lorton** (this is a good place to take a break, because there's a very big climb ahead up Whinlatter).

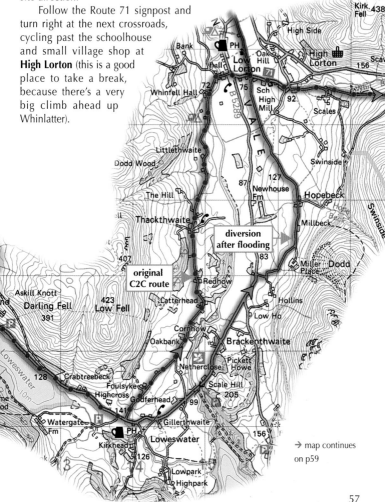

→ map continues on p59

Start of the climb from High Lorton past Scales Farm towards Whinlatter Pass

There is a good choice of **accommodation** in and around High and Low Lorton, ranging from the luxurious Winder Hall, Old Vicarage or New House Farm to more modest B&Bs. This delightful area is well worth exploring, with high hills to the west, the lowlands of Lorton Vale to the east and excellent walks.
    More information *www.dalesandvales.co.uk*

Just past the shop, take the second turning on the right and follow a narrow lane past **Boonbeck** and **Scales**, where Swinside End Farm (www.swinsideendfarm. co.uk) could be a good choice for a pre-Whinlatter B&B, ensuring that you are fully fuelled to tackle that big hill first thing in the morning. This is where the fun starts. It's not a bad hill, but be prepared for a long, steady climb which will add about 200 vertical metres to your C2C trip. On the plus side, you are riding through beautiful countryside and are unlikely to meet cars. There is a convenient bench about halfway up the hill, which is a great place to take in panoramic views to the west – with luck it will be a fine day! Keep on riding uphill, then enjoy more level pedalling by the side of **Blaze Beck** on what is pleasingly described by the local signpost as a 'Narrow Gated Road'. Not far on, the C2C route joins the **B5292** by **Blaze Bridge** below Lorton Fells. The short ride along the B5292 is usually enjoyable and stress-free, with the benefit of almost zero traffic. But you need to take care when crossing this road at the entry and exit junctions, just in case.

The C2C follows the B5292 for less than 1.5km (1 mile) of easy riding, before it's time to turn right into the parking area at **Swinside House**, which is clearly signposted as part of the route just after a patch of conifers on the left. At this point, you'll be pleased if you are riding a mountain bike, as the next 5km (3 miles) are nearly all off-road on forest tracks, following Whinlatter Pass and descending through Whinlatter Forest to the side of Bassenthwaite Lake. Those on a hybrid or touring bike should be fine. The tracks are all pretty good – not tricky or bumpy until the last stage. If you are riding a skinny-tyre racing bike, it would be better to continue on the road, which will also provide a pleasant (and much quicker) ride towards Keswick.

The forestry track runs parallel to the road, providing a pleasant if unremarkable ride through **Whinlatter Pass** with fairly gentle ups and downs. It leads to a small car park by the road at **Comb Bridge**, where you may need to take a little care with navigation. It is easy to miss the C2C signpost and chose what appears to be the logical option of turning downhill. This provides a much shorter and considerably quicker route to Braithwaite, but misses out a great chunk of the correct C2C route. So instead, you need

→ map continues on p62

Workington route joins

to turn left onto the road and start pedalling uphill. Thankfully, it's only a short distance before a turn right (take care) into the main entrance for **Whinlatter Forest Park and Visitor Centre**. Be warned, this place is popular

WELCOME TO THE WOODS

C2C signpost leads straight past the visitor centre and bike shop at Whinlatter Forest Country Park

Whinlatter Forest Park claims to be England's only true mountain forest, rising to 790m above sea level, with fine views across the Lake District and towards Scotland.

Specially built trails for mountain bikers combine stunning views with great single-track riding that leads to a high point 500m above Keswick. The red-grade Altura Trail covers 19km (11¾ miles) including 15km (9¼ miles) of single track with berms, jumps, rocks, cork screws and table tops for experienced riders, with fine views of Derwent Water, Bassenthwaite, Helvellyn and Skiddaw. The less demanding blue-grade Quercus Trail covers 7.5km (4½ miles) with a shorter 3.5km (2 mile) option, featuring flowing single-track riding with gentle berms, rolling jumps and gradual climbs. Both trails start from the Whinlatter Visitor Centre, where there is a bike shop run by Cyclewise, café, bike wash and bike hire.

Go Ape! is an award-winning, high-wire forest adventure course of extreme rope bridges, Tarzan swings and zip slides, trekking from tree to tree in the forest canopy 12m above the forest floor. Additional attractions include watching the Bassenthwaite ospreys through a live nest camera, while learning about the Lake District Osprey Project.

More information www.forestry.gov.uk

Beautiful spot for a picnic on the long trail through Whinlatter Forest

during holidays and may be busy with cars.

Ride past the zip wire that leads into the Go Ape! course and continue past the Cyclewise bike shop at the Forest Centre, where you pick up a sign for Route 71 of the C2C. Some cyclists may like to take time out to sample the Altura or Quercus mountain bike trails, which are highly rated by those who enjoy a single-track challenge. The C2C route goes its own way, following the main forest track downhill through a series of bends. Follow the C2C signposts to a left turn, which brings you to a delightful picnic spot with a shady bench by the side of a small lake and tumbling waterfall – the perfect place to eat sandwiches on a sunny day.

The C2C route continues downhill on forestry tracks with good surfaces for hybrid or mountain-bike tyres. It's a fairly gentle descent, which is just as well should you shoot round a corner and meet a couple of pram pushers or dog walkers. The track gets narrower as it heads down a particularly attractive section cut into the hillside, with fine views opening out towards the south-west and Derwent Water. From here, the track dips more steeply downhill, with glimpses of Bassenthwaite,

Whinlatter Forest tracks leading towards the base of the fells by Bassenthwaite Lake

heading down to a rough tarmac lane at **Thornthwaite**, where you follow the C2C signpost with a sharp turn to the right. Ride a short distance to join a minor road with a three-way C2C signpost for Keswick, Cockermouth or Whitehaven. **The C2C route from Workington via Cockermouth joins the route here.**

Take the Keswick direction and ride straight ahead, following the old road parallel to the new A66, with its high-speed traffic. By contrast, the C2C provides a leisurely, pleasant ride towards the village of **Braithwaite**, with a fine backdrop of Grisedale, Causey Pike, High Stile and Barrow forming the Coledale Horseshoe.

Braithwaite would be a good place to stop overnight for those who don't fancy the hustle and bustle of nearby Keswick. There is a good choice of accommodation (*www.dalesandvales.co.uk*) and places to eat and drink, with excellent walking right on the doorstep.

Anyone interested in industrial history should follow the footpath alongside Coledale Beck to Force Crag Mine, the last working metal mine in the Lake District, which has been restored by the National Trust. Allow 2hrs walking, plus time to see the buildings and machinery (although you are not allowed to go inside or down the mine).

At Braithwaite, Route 71 crosses straight over the **B5292** and follows a minor undulating road heading south-west past a large camp site to **Little Braithwaite**, crossing Newlands Beck and continuing via **Ullock** and **Derwent Bank** to join the **B5289** on the western outskirts of **Keswick**. Here there is a shared path on the pavement for walkers and cyclists, which is fine for as long as it lasts. You can follow a path that cuts out part of the road, but the final approach is a straight choice between riding on a fairly busy road or pushing along the pavement. This is one of the least cycle-friendly sections of the entire C2C route, in spite of the fact that there appears to be plenty of space to build a decent cycle path right into the centre of town.

KESWICK

The market town of Keswick is one of the Lake District's major honeypots. The town is interesting, although most of the old shops have been replaced by innumerable stores selling outdoor hiking gear – you have never seen so many boots in your life! There are lots of pubs and cafés serving the many tourists. It is pleasant to stroll around the pedestrianised centre, which is dominated by the splendid Moot Hall and is the perfect place to buy outdoor wear. There is a huge choice of B&Bs in quiet side streets and

The C2C route passes within a few metres of Keswick's fine market place

plenty to occupy your time, with superb walking from the town that ranges from strolling along the shore of Derwent Water (on which you can take a cruise) to long hikes on the high fells.

Cyclists will enjoy a visit to the Lakeland Pedlar (www.lakelandpedlar. co.uk) at Bell Close on the edge of the town's Bank Street car park, just behind the main shopping precinct and close to Cotswold Leisure. It combines an excellent whole-food café, which is perfect for cyclists, with a cycle shop run by Keswick Bikes, who also have an mountain-bike shop and a hire centre and workshop at Main Street, in Keswick (www.keswickbikes.co.uk).

More information www.keswick.org

LINK ROUTE

ST BEES TO THE C2C

Distance	4km (2½ miles)
Time	20mins
Ascent	120m
Descent	56m
Start	St Bees railway station, GR119970
Access by road	7.4km (4½ miles) south of Whitehaven on the B5346
Access by rail	On the West Cumbria railway line run by Northern Trains (tel: 0845 600 11 59), connecting Carlisle to Lancaster via Workington, Whitehaven and Barrow-in-Furness. The railway station is within easy reach of the village and all its amenities.
Accommodation	The village website provides useful information on hotels and B&B. Fairladies Barn (www.fairladiesbarn.co.uk), a converted 17th-century sandstone barn on Main Street, provides decent accommodation, a good breakfast and friendly service, as well as long-term car parking at modest cost. Pubs, hotels and cafés are within easy reach for dinner. Try the Manor House in Main Street for an unpretentious dinner at reasonable cost in relaxed surroundings.
More information	www.stbees.org.uk

It's not part of the official C2C route, but starting from St Bees provides an interesting option. St Bees is a rambling village a few miles south of Whitehaven, with a wide sandy beach at low water and attractive walks around St Bees Head. Apart from being a pleasant place for relaxed seaside holidays, St Bees' main claim to fame is being the start point of Alfred Wainwright's coast-to-coast walk, a 307km (191 mile) marathon ending at Robin Hood's Bay in North Yorkshire.

For cyclists, the main attraction is that St Bees is a lot smaller and quieter than Whitehaven and provides an enjoyable, stress-free link to the C2C with surprisingly good road and rail connections. The principal disadvantage of starting here is that it means missing the first 6.5km (4 miles) of the C2C and getting your card stamped at the start. Accommodation may be limited if there is a large influx of walkers.

The link between St Bees and the C2C is easy to navigate and provides an enjoyable warm-up at the start of the ride. From the **railway station**, follow the **B5345** south for a short distance, riding towards the main part of the village. Take the first left turn and head out of the village, following this quiet road as it curves in a north-easterly direction. A moderately stiff uphill brings you to **High House**, after which there are fine views across the flood plain, with the railway snaking along the side of the valley towards Whitehaven.

Keep following the road through pleasant countryside, with easy ups and downs leading past **High Walton**, **Low Walton**, **Low Walton Wood** and **Linethwaite**. Having passed woodland on the right, look out for a path on the left side of the road leading down to the disused railway line close to **Scalegill**. If you reach the busy A595, you have overshot the turn-off, which is just to the west of the road bridge. Go down to join the C2C railway path and ride under the **A595**.

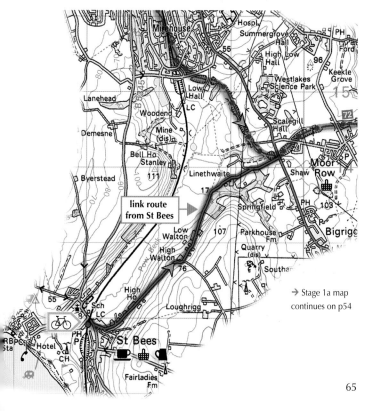

→ Stage 1a map
continues on p54

65

STAGE 1B

WORKINGTON TO KESWICK

Distance	39km (24 miles)
Time	3–5hrs
Ascent	613m
Descent	533m
Start	Mini-lighthouse, Workington old port, GR297982

The C2C route from Workington to Keswick is shorter, easier and less popular than Whitehaven to Keswick. It also has less dramatic scenery, but scores with a visit to Cockermouth, followed by a fine ride towards Bassenthwaite Lake.

The start/finish of the C2C is well hidden in Workington. It's in a bleak position by the mini-lighthouse looking over the Irish Sea, connected via a promontory to the old port and well outside the town, but within easy reach of Workington's railway station, located near the head of the river port.

From the **lighthouse**, turn your back on the Irish Sea and ride towards Workington, with the estuary on your left. Follow the C2C signs past the small **yacht harbour** and **inner port**, which has been attractively landscaped and would be a lovely place to stop on a fine day. The route is clearly signposted through a large car park, where it goes up a

Workington's start (or finish) of the C2C

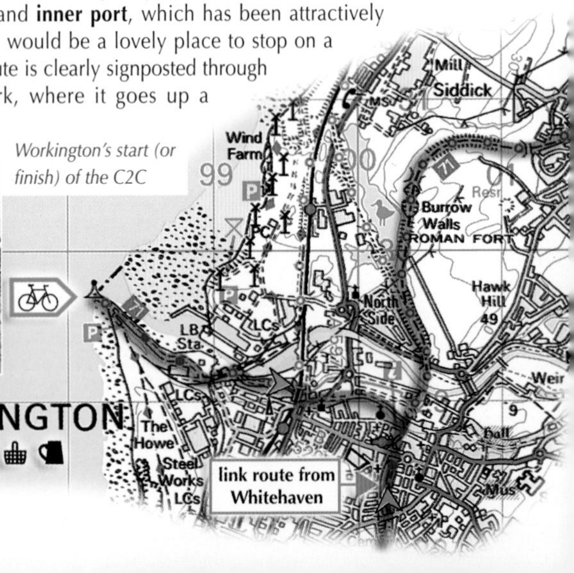

link route from Whitehaven

WORKINGTON

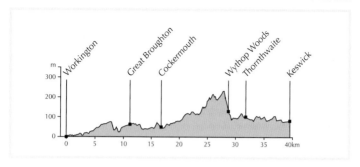

narrow path on the right side. This is clearly a walkway, so pushing your bike seems sensible. Ride past a few modern shops with a fine old building on the left. Before you know it, you're on the outskirts of Workington, riding downhill towards the **River Derwent**.

Sadly, Workington had huge problems in the floods of November 2009. The river burst its banks with such force that the fine old bridge collapsed in ruins. Consequently, the C2C was diverted to a temporary bridge for cyclists and walkers 200m upstream, where the direction of the route is quite confusing. The solution is to turn left downriver as far as the old bridge, then go up a short track, cross straight over a roundabout and look for the **Hagworm Wiggle Pass** bridge, which crosses the road and marks the start of a railway path with a good tarmac surface for enjoyable car-free riding all the way to Camerton, via North Side and Seaton, 8km (5 miles) from the start of the C2C.

→ map continues on p68

Start of the C2C cycle path at Hagworm Wiggle Pass

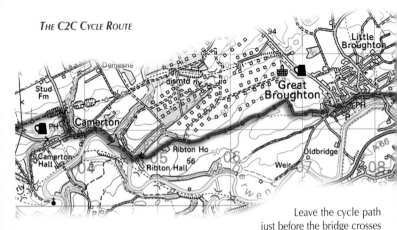

Leave the cycle path just before the bridge crosses the railway path at **Uplands**, turning right on the road and heading steeply downhill into **Camerton**. Be careful here – the road sweeps round to the right and it's easy to overshoot the C2C, which turns sharp left onto a narrow lane. From here the C2C follows an undulating route through peaceful countryside towards Cockermouth, with a few short, sharp ups and downs before **Great Broughton**, where you may like to pause at the Punchbowl pub before riding on to Cockermouth.

Ride downhill into **Cockermouth** and follow the C2C sign to the right at the next T-junction. This leads across the river, where there is the choice of turning left into the town or right to continue direct to Keswick. The latter provides a simple and effective bypass route. Having crossed the bridge, turn right away from the town, then immediately left to follow a C2C signpost and join a tarmac cycle track along the south side of Cockermouth. Cross over a main road after a car park (turn right to go down into the town from here) and join the track that continues

COCKERMOUTH

The town suffered widespread damage when the River Cocker and River Derwent flooded in November 2009, but its fine old buildings have steadily been restored. Unlike some of the region's honeypot centres, Cockermouth has not been overwhelmed by tourism and still retains the feel of an attractive market town, which is pleasant to explore with the Civic Trust Town Trail as a guide. The top attraction is Dorothy and William Wordsworth's Georgian house in Main Street, which is run by the National Trust. Some C2C riders may prefer a tour of nearby Jennings Brewery!

More information www.cockermouth.org.uk

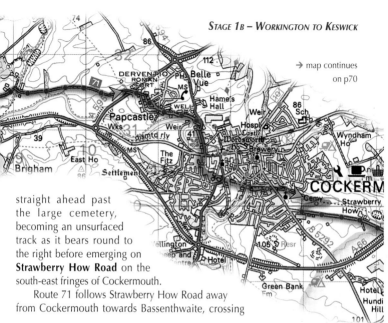

→ map continues on p70

straight ahead past the large cemetery, becoming an unsurfaced track as it bears round to the right before emerging on **Strawberry How Road** on the south-east fringes of Cockermouth.

Route 71 follows Strawberry How Road away from Cockermouth towards Bassenthwaite, crossing

Start of long and highly enjoyable offroad section near Wythop Hall

69

Following field tracks towards Wythop Woods

over the **A66** and bearing left to head due east. Follow this fairly quiet country road in the direction of Wythop Mill, enjoying views of the fells ahead with gentle ups and downs through the undulating

→ Stage 1a map continues on p62

landscape. At **Hall Bank** the route bears right onto a narrow lane, then right again below **Ling Fell**, passing **Eskin** and **Old Scales**, with superb views towards Scale Fell. This is a dead-end road, so you are unlikely to meet motor traffic. It's also a wonderful place to ride. Just by the entrance to **Wythop Hall**, the C2C route goes off-road, following a clear track across green fields and turning right by the entrance to **Lowthwaite Farm**. This section is extremely enjoyable in dry weather, but in the wet could become a muddy ride.

The C2C route joins a narrow track that leads steeply down into **Wythop Woods**. This is proper mountain-bike terrain and quite challenging.

71

Enjoying the view of Bassenthwaite Lake, before resuming the descent

You might get down on a hybrid, but it will be easier to walk some of the steeper, rougher sections. The narrow track soon levels out along the side of the hill, with tantalising glimpses of Bassenthwaite Lake through the trees. It's an exhilarating and highly enjoyable ride down to the lakeside – a lot more interesting than the alternative descent from Whinlatter (Stage 1a). Eventually, the route drops down by the side of the **A66**.

Thankfully an ancient hidden lane leads through the fringes of the woods and joins a quiet road by a parking place at **Woodend Brow**, which still runs parallel to the A66. Ride on for a mile or so past **Powter How**, then look out for a three-way signpost on the right indicating the junction of the Whitehaven and Workington C2C routes. Turn to Stage 1a (page 62) to follow the route to Keswick.

LINK ROUTE

WHITEHAVEN TO WORKINGTON

Distance	14.5km (9 miles)
Time	1hr 15mins
Ascent	152m
Descent	144m
Start	Whitehaven harbour, GR182971

Hadrian's Cycleway (Route 72) links Whitehaven to Workington, the two optional start/finish points of the C2C on the west coast. Most of the route is traffic-free and follows level ground, with only one moderate hill climb. For more information on Whitehaven see Stage 1a.

Route 72 is clearly signposted in Whitehaven **harbour**, close to the steel pillar marking the start/finish of the C2C. Beyond the harbour, turn inland and bear left around the Texaco filling station. At this point the route is neither obvious nor cycle-friendly, particularly as you appear to be heading steeply uphill. But don't worry – the traffic-free cycle path follows the sea wall by the side of the single-line railway, which is a delightful ride on a fine day. Route 72 turns inland at **Parton**, where it joins the road and provides the sole moderate hill climb.

Near the top of the hill, turn right onto a rough track clearly signposted as Route 72. This feeds into a tarmac cycle track that goes all the way to **Workington** and is very easy to ride. Route 72 runs through to the North Side of Workington, where it runs together with Route 71 (C2C) for a short distance, before the C2C peels off towards Cockermouth.

Riding along the sea wall, following the Hadrian's Wall route north out of Whitehaven

STAGE 2

KESWICK TO LANGWATHBY

Distance	46km (28½ miles)
Time	4–5hrs
Ascent	597m
Descent	578m
Start	Moot Hall, Keswick, GR235267

The C2C follows a wonderful railway path out of Keswick and continues in shadow of Blencathra before leaving the north-eastern fringes of the Lake District National Park, looking towards the Pennines as it continues through Penrith to the village of Langwathby.

From the Moot Hall in the pedestrianised centre of **Keswick**, follow Station Street into Station Road, then turn left towards the Keswick Leisure Pool and Fitness Centre. The C2C route is not particularly clear here, but a tarmac path leads to a car park by Keswick's fine old railway station, which is now part of the hotel nearby.

By the old station find the start of the **Keswick Railway Footpath**, which provides a delightful 6.5km (4 mile) stretch of traffic-free cycling on the C2C. This is part of the former Cockermouth, Keswick and Penrith Railway, which closed as recently as 1972. The 29km (18 miles) of railway between Penrith and Keswick included 78 bridges, but sadly much of the route was obliterated by 'improvements' to the A66.

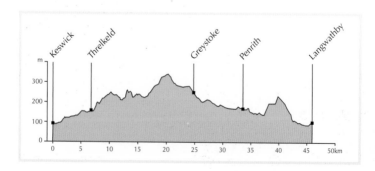

The Keswick Railway Footpath follows the course of the River Greta and provides a delightful cycle route

The Keswick Railway Footpath is popular for walkers and families with young children wobbling on bikes, so please keep your speed under control. Take time to enjoy the splendid section of aerial walkway crossing the Greta Gorge, the superb views of the River Greta tumbling downstream as you cycle across eight fine bridges, and information plaques telling the story of the railway's history, the River Greta, the local bobbin industry and natural history – watch out for red squirrels.

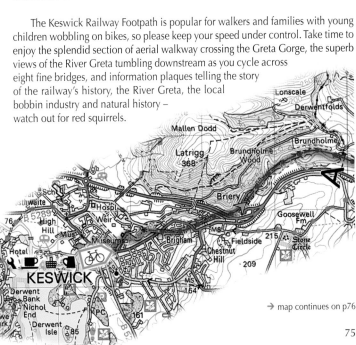

→ map continues on p76

75

It's sad to leave this delightful railway path, which is cut off by the everyday reality of thundering traffic on the **A66**. Thankfully, cyclists have to ride along the pavement by the side of this road only for a few metres before peeling off to follow a fairly quiet road through the village of **Threlkeld** beneath mighty Blencathra or 'Saddleback', towering above at 866m. The Horse & Farrier Inn could be a pleasant place to stop for a pint, with benches in front and fine views across the valley towards Helvellyn, providing a welcome respite before the C2C rejoins the **A66**. It's relatively stress-free riding on the pavement, but a great relief to turn off after almost 1.5km (1 mile) and ride past the White Horse Inn at **Scales**, which at the time of writing was closed due to flooding.

From Scales the C2C route improves dramatically, turning north towards Mungrisdale on a narrow, gated lane that skirts the fells. Watch out for 'Slow Down!' signs on the downhill approach to **Southerfell Farm** – cyclists who don't follow this advice will ride slap-bang into a closed gate round a blind bend. This is a very pleasant section of the C2C, with fine views to the south amid quiet surroundings beneath Blencathra. At the **Mill Inn**, beside the River Glenderamackin close to Mungrisdale, there are two choices. Either turn right and follow the signpost for Route 71 back to the A66, which means following close by the side of this busy main road for over 3km (2 miles) before turning north at the Sportsman Inn towards Nobles Farm; or turn left and follow the alternative route on the link to Reivers Cycle Route 10. The latter option is recommended and described below.

Follow the narrow, winding road north through the quaint hamlet of **Mungrisdale** below Bowscale Fell in superb surroundings. Take the first right turn after the chapel, leaving the Reivers Route to head north-east past the farmstead at **Mossdyke** and enjoying easy level riding on

→ map continues on p78

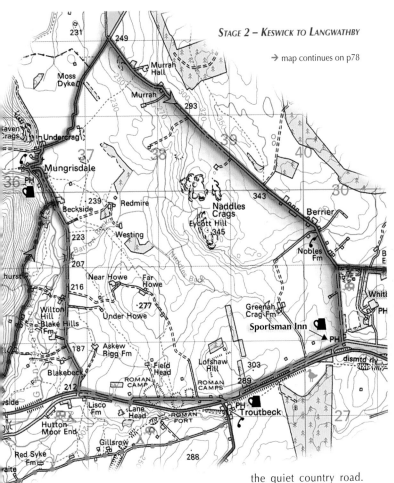

the quiet country road.

At the next crossroads turn right for **Murrah** and Berrier, but take time to stop and look back at the superb view of the eastern edge of the Lakeland fells, which appear to plunge down from the sky.

Unfortunately, there is no such thing as a free meal. The long section of straight road ahead goes steadily uphill. It's not much of a gradient, but the nearly 5km (3 miles) climb feels like a long grind in bad weather, which makes it a relief to spot the next C2C signpost after **Berrier**. Turn left for **Greystoke** and enjoy an easy downhill most of the way to the ancestral home of Tarzan.

For cyclists in picnic mode, there's a nicely placed bench by a wall on the left as you ride into the village. Anyone in pint-of-beer mode can pay a visit to the **Boot & Shoe pub** on the C2C route through the village. Alternatively, try Greystoke's superb Cycle Café Tea Garden on the way out of the village.

North-east of Greystoke, the C2C follows quiet roads and gentle hills on the route towards Penrith, with views opening out towards the Pennines. Ride

GREYSTOKE CYCLE CAFÉ

Greystoke Cycle Café is a lovely place to visit, right next door to Greystoke Castle, where Tarzan 'King of the Apes' was (supposedly) born and bred. It's a family-run establishment that favours cyclists arriving on bikes.

The Tea Garden is delightful and the food is excellent, but it opens only

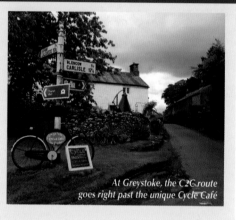

At Greystoke, the C2C route goes right past the unique Cycle Café

from Easter to the end of September (12–6pm on Fridays, 10am–6pm on Saturdays and 10am–6pm on the second Sunday of each month). The adjacent Cyclists' Barn is open until the end of October (9.30am–6pm every day), then closed until Easter, and sells self-service hot drinks, cold drinks and flapjacks to C2C cyclists. It also provides interesting things to read and basic tools to fix punctures and other bike problems, and offers a garden area that can be used for camping.

In addition, the Cycle Café runs an interesting range of 'Quirky Workshops' (or 'Take a day off from the C2C courses'), with local accommodation and the possibility of daily transport to different parts of the C2C.

Note There is no parking for cars apart from cycle-support vehicles. Motorists are welcome to enjoy the food and atmosphere, but have to walk 300m from the village car park.

More information www.greystokecyclecafe.co.uk

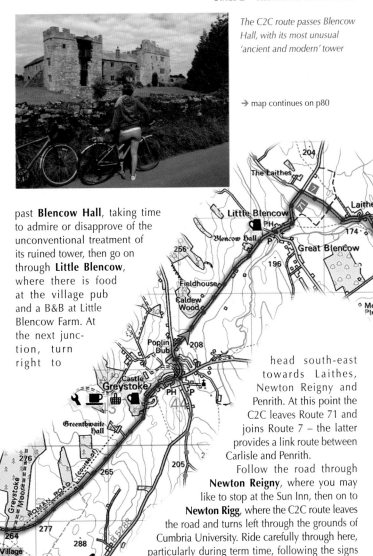

The C2C route passes Blencow Hall, with its most unusual 'ancient and modern' tower

→ map continues on p80

past **Blencow Hall**, taking time to admire or disapprove of the unconventional treatment of its ruined tower, then go on through **Little Blencow**, where there is food at the village pub and a B&B at Little Blencow Farm. At the next junction, turn right to head south-east towards Laithes, Newton Reigny and Penrith. At this point the C2C leaves Route 71 and joins Route 7 – the latter provides a link route between Carlisle and Penrith.

Follow the road through **Newton Reigny**, where you may like to stop at the Sun Inn, then on to **Newton Rigg**, where the C2C route leaves the road and turns left through the grounds of Cumbria University. Ride carefully through here, particularly during term time, following the signs

On the road to Langwathby, with the impressive barrier of the Pennines looming larger with every pedal stroke

between buildings to a track that leads downhill towards the M6 motorway, with Penrith beyond. Follow this track through the underpass to the outskirts of **Penrith**, where you are directed along a cycle path alongside **Drovers Lane**, heading the 'wrong way' down a one-way street. This route provides a good

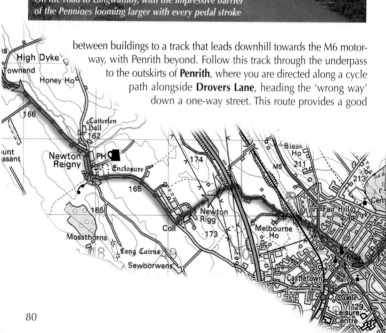

way to bypass the town – it continues straight ahead past a church on **Meeting House Lane**, where it becomes a two-way street until it reaches the roundabout where the eastbound C2C signpost (Route 7) points left uphill. (If you want to go into town, turn right down the hill. As Penrith is not particularly cycle-friendly, it is advisable to push your bike to the centre, which is about 5mins walk.)

Heading eastwards on the C2C, there is a stiff climb up **Fell Lane**. At the top turn right along **Beacon Edge**, following the escarpment of Beacon Fell, with huge views to the south. The road then tips down and it seems like the start of an amazing downhill. Unfortunately, the C2C turns left soon after you get up speed, so watch for the signpost and be ready to pull on the brakes.

Follow the undulating country lane in a north-easterly direction. After an uphill introduction, it gets better and better, with some great swooping downhill sections and more fine views of the Pennines. The C2C turns left for a short ride along the **B6412**, which is reasonably cycle-friendly, then right along another country lane before joining the **A686** in the final approach to **Langwathby**. A-roads are

81

seldom attractive for cyclists, but this short section is reasonably stress-free, with the bonus of a segregated bridge for walkers and cyclists over the River Eden.

LANGWATHBY

Langwathby village green, with the Shepherds Inn perfectly located for a lunchtime drink

The village of Langwathby has a pleasant green, with a war memorial directly on the C2C route, swings for children, benches for picnics and the friendly Shepherds Inn for ale. The nearest accommodation appears to be at Bank House Farm (www.bankhouseequestrian.co.uk) in Little Salkeld, just over 3km (2 miles) past Langwathby on the C2C route, which welcomes cyclists and offers B&B, self-catering and camping facilities. For those who prefer to go upmarket there is Edenhall Country Hotel & Restaurant (www. edenhallhotel.co.uk) on the south side of Langwathby. On the third Sunday in May, children dance run the maypole on the village green, celebrating the rite of spring. C2C riders who like animals should allow time to visit Eden Ostrich World (www.ostrich-world.com) at Langwathby Hall Farm, a working farm with black ostriches and other curious animals for great family fun.

STAGE 3

LANGWATHBY TO NENTHEAD

Distance	35km (21½ miles)
Time	4–5hrs
Ascent	977m
Descent	631m
Start	War memorial, Langwathby village green, GR336568

The C2C leaves the Lake District behind as it heads towards the low, rising hills of the Pennines, steadily climbing towards Hartside before plunging down towards Alston and Garrigill, with a final long climb towards Nenthead.

Turn left by the memorial to follow Route 7 in a northerly direction. This leads out of **Langwathby** on a fairly quiet road parallel to the railway, crossing under a bridge by Eden Mount and arriving at **Little Salkeld**, where you might like to visit the gaily painted watermill.

> **Little Salkeld Watermill** is a working mill with tearoom, bread-making courses, bakery, mill shop and gallery in a picturesque stetting. Open daily 10.30am–5pm throughout the year (except Christmas to mid-January).
> **More information** www.organicmill.co.uk

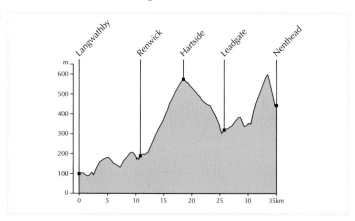

A sharp uphill from the watermill gives a taster of the ups and downs ahead, which become more commonplace and a little strength-sapping. Take time out from the C2C to visit the stone circle known as Long Meg and Her Daughters by taking the next left turn. It's less than the ½ mile (800m) shown on the signpost, and the remote, little visited site is a great place for a picnic in half-decent weather.

> **Long Meg and Her Daughters** form the second biggest stone circle in England, and are thought to date from around 1500BC. Long Meg is the tallest of 69 stones, standing 3.7m high, decorated with three mysterious symbols and having four corners facing the points of the compass. Long Meg is local red sandstone, while her daughters are rhyolite granite. Local legend claims that Meg was a witch who was turned to stone with her daughter for profaning the Sabbath, while they danced wildly upon the moor. It is said that it is impossible to count the same number of stones twice, without breaking the magic of the circle.

Ride on along Route 7, following a very quiet country lane in beautiful surroundings, with imposing views of the unbroken chain of Pennines that gradually looms nearer the C2C. Watch out for the pick-your-own fruit farm on the left side, which provides a pleasant break from riding when raspberries are in season, and also

The Pennines get closer as the C2C leads along quiet, undulating lanes towards Renwick – this is superb cycling through beautiful countryside where motor traffic is rare

watch for the llama farm, where these curious creatures provide an alternative view. The C2C turns north as it follows the swooping, undulating lanes towards Renwick. At **Four Lane End**, come to a crossroads with the Route 7 sign pointing straight ahead for Alston (on-road) or right for Alston (off-road). Turn right if you have a mountain bike and enjoy the challenge of tackling a long uphill on a rough track. Those with any kind of road bike should go straight ahead and follow the narrow road as it zooms downhill and weaves across Renwick Bridge,

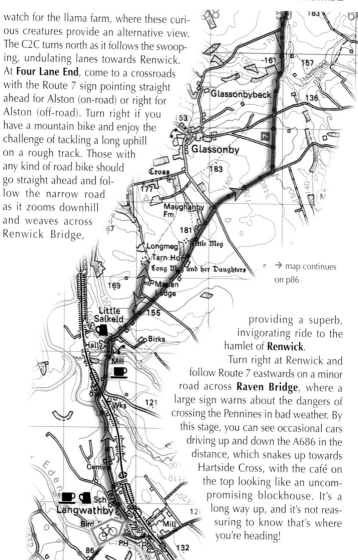

→ map continues on p86

providing a superb, invigorating ride to the hamlet of **Renwick**.

Turn right at Renwick and follow Route 7 eastwards on a minor road across **Raven Bridge**, where a large sign warns about the dangers of crossing the Pennines in bad weather. By this stage, you can see occasional cars driving up and down the A686 in the distance, which snakes up towards Hartside Cross, with the café on the top looking like an uncompromising blockhouse. It's a long way up, and it's not reassuring to know that's where you're heading!

85

The road provides a long but steady uphill in remote, quiet surroundings where you're unlikely to meet other vehicles. Just beyond a large house in a splendidly isolated position at **Selah**, the C2C on-road and off-road routes are reunited, but there is another decision to make about the route. The road route bears round to the south-east as it winds quite steeply uphill to join the **A686**, on which you have to put up with all the passing traffic on the 1.5km (1 mile) or more to the top of the hill. For cyclists who want to get to the top quickly, that's the way to go. However, if it's a nice day and you want to make the most of a magnificent panorama to the north across the wild landscape of Haresceugh Fell, try the off-road route (described below). It will take a lot longer and you will need to push for most of the second half, even on a mountain bike, but in spite of the exertion it is worth the effort (anyone with full camping gear should keep to the road route).

For the **off-road route**, follow the track straight ahead, through a gate by a ruined building and down towards a bridge, where the track can become very muddy. After that, a very steep uphill across

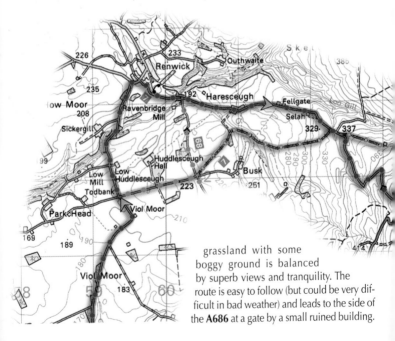

grassland with some boggy ground is balanced by superb views and tranquility. The route is easy to follow (but could be very difficult in bad weather) and leads to the side of the **A686** at a gate by a small ruined building.

Once you have crossed the gill, the off-road route to Hartside gets more challenging and becomes very steep

→ map continues on p88

Cross straight over and continue to push up (or ride if you are tough) the old ruined road that goes direct to the top of **Hartside**, passing one of many elegant C2C 'artisan' signposts.

The routes rejoin at **Hartside Top Café**, which sits right on top of the hill and is a favourite meeting place for bikers with big engines. On a busy weekend, there are hundreds of shiny motorbikes up there, which will hopefully not be blasting up and down the Alston road. With no reason to stop, hop on your bike and continue on the longest A-road section of the entire C2C. Thankfully, the 6.5km (4 mile) descent is all downhill on a long, steady gradient. Watch out for the turn-off signposted to Leadgate and Garrigill, just as the A686 bends round to the left. This is a potentially dangerous junction, where it may be wise to pull into the side, get off your bike and push across to the Leadgate road.

There is a beautiful downhill to **Leadgate**, where cyclists turn either right at a road junction to follow Route 7 or left if they wish to divert to **Alston** on Route 68, which follows the valley of the River South Tyne with an easy 3km (2 mile) ride into the centre of this delightful small market town. (To rejoin the east-bound C2C from Alston, ride up the main street to join the A689, then bear left onto the B6277 heading south from the town. Follow this road for just over 3km (2 miles) past the Alston Training and Adventure Centre, and fork right onto a lane leading down to Garrigill as the B6277 bends left.)

ALSTON

Alston claims to be the highest market settlement in England and is totally surrounded by Pennine landscape within an Area of Outstanding Natural Beauty. The steep main street is cobbled, which does an excellent job of slowing down traffic, and has a fine market cross and splendid buildings dating from the 17th century. There are several pubs and a few pleasant shops, including the excellent Moody Baker (www.themoodybaker.co.uk) in the High Street. There is a good choice of accommodation in and around the town – Alston House (www.alstonhouse.co.uk), near the centre, is comfortable and welcomes cyclists. No visit to Alston would be complete without a ride on the South Tynedale Railway. England's highest narrow-gauge railway puffs its way from Alston station (267m/875ft above sea level) to Kirkhaugh, following part of the old Haltwhistle to Alston branch line. It's only 3km (2 miles), but is a delightful trip, and you can walk back to Alston along the Pennine Way.

From the road junction at **Leadgate**, the C2C heads steeply down to **Blackburn Bridge** then steeply up the other side, passing through places with such memorable names as **Slaggieburn** and **Shake Holes** below Rotherhope Fell. It then dives down to the attractive village of **Garrigill**, with its post office beside the green, although its pub was boarded and shut at the time of writing.

There are two C2C routes out of Garrigill. The road route (described below) goes direct to Nenthead. The off-road route follows a southern loop that almost doubles the distance, with some steep climbing and rough riding past quarries

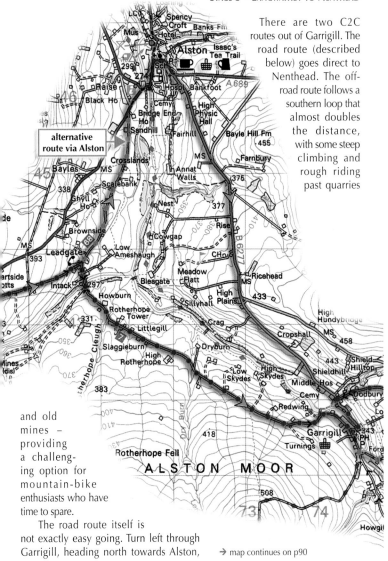

and old mines – providing a challenging option for mountain-bike enthusiasts who have time to spare.

The road route itself is not exactly easy going. Turn left through Garrigill, heading north towards Alston,

→ map continues on p90

89

THE C2C CYCLE ROUTE

then right by **Low Houses Bridge**, where you can pause to admire the rather splendid waterfalls by a

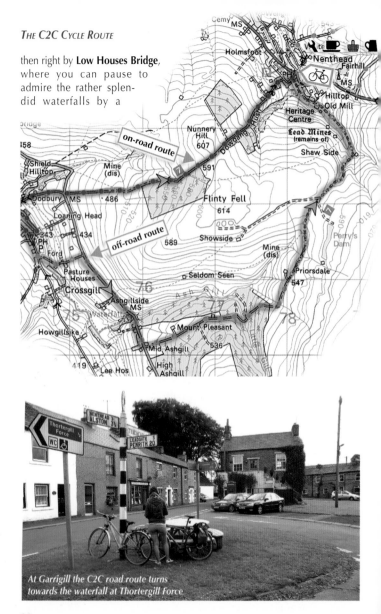

At Garrigill the C2C road route turns towards the waterfall at Thortergill Force

Just past the brow of this hill, the road down into Nenthead gets seriously steep with tight bends – a bicycle black spot!

converted chapel. Hit this next hill with conviction – it is the steepest, toughest climb on the eastbound C2C. If you can pedal to the top, well done! The bad news is that the real top is still 3km (2 miles) away. It's like a mirage, with each top succeeded by another top as you steadily gain height on **Alston Moor**. The scenery is very fine, and it's not such a bad climb with a following wind, but it could be really miserable in poor weather and rain.

It's a great relief to pass a large area of forestry and bridge the crest at **Nunnery Hill**. From here, there is a very fast downhill into **Nenthead**, spread out below. Take note of the 'Go Slow! Bicycle Accident Black Spot!' signs on the bends. The last part of the hill gets seriously steep and needs to be treated with maximum respect. You may, at this point, choose to get off and push your bike downhill.

NENTHEAD

Nenthead is a pretty little place, in spite of starting life as a purpose-built industrial village in the mid-18th century servicing major lead and silver mines. Nenthead Mines Heritage Centre (www.npht.com) provides a comprehensive history of mining in the North Pennines on its 200-acre site, with exhibitions and activities including trips down the mine and mineral panning, together with bunkhouse accommodation, a picnic area and café at the bottom of Slate Hill, which has been recommended by riders tackling the C2C.

Other attractions at Nenthead include the Miners Arms (www.nenthead.com), a traditional 18th-century pub and official C2C stamping post right in the village centre that offers restaurant and accommodation ideally situated for a C2C stop-over. Next door is North Pennine Cycles, providing a service to cyclists at 'the heart of the C2C', and next to this Nenthead Community Shop and post office, which sells snacks and ice cream.

STAGE 4

NENTHEAD TO CONSETT

Distance	48km (30 miles)
Time	3–4hrs
Ascent	804m
Descent	991m
Start	Nenthead, GR437782

Little more than 1.5km (1 mile) to the east of Nenthead is the highest point of the C2C. This is the start of a long and splendid downhill through beautiful wild country – very quiet, remote and with luck totally car free. Welcome to Northumberland, England's 'Border Country'.

On leaving Nenthead to the east, there are two options. For those looking for a quick passage, the C2C road route starts with a short, but fairly steep climb on the **A689** (normally pretty quiet for an A-road) out of Nenthead, signposted as Route 7 to Allenheads. Take the first left turn by old mine workings to join a minor road heading north, crossing Gillgill Burn while continuing the climb up **Black Hill** to 609m above sea level – the highest point of the C2C.

Alternatively, for those who don't mind rough riding, the off-road route is more direct, quieter and provides superb views to the west. Past

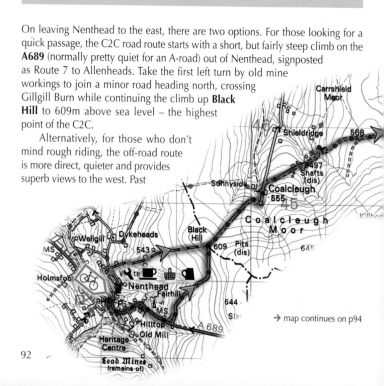

→ map continues on p94

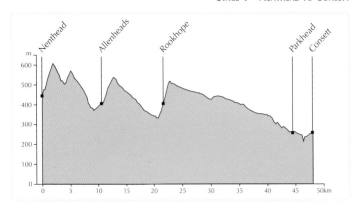

the Miners Arms and North Pennine Cycles, take the left turning uphill by the side of **Nenthead Community Shop**. There is no signpost here, but if the tarmac soon becomes cobbles, you are on the correct route and will be pedalling steeply uphill. Just as you feel your lungs might burst reach the delightfully old-fashioned Victorian primary **school**. Turn 90° right here onto a **tarmac lane**, which soon turns 90° left past a row of houses.

The bridleway track leading up to the top of **Black Hill** is a little further on and clearly signposted. It's not particularly steep and is easy enough to tackle with enthusiasm on a mountain bike. A hybrid will be harder, but the track surface is

The off-road route above Nenthead leads to Black Hill and the highest point of the C2C – the track here is in good condition, with superb views and fabulous surroundings

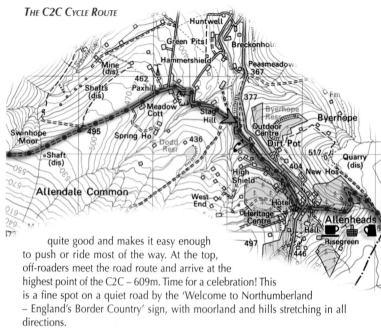

quite good and makes it easy enough to push or ride most of the way. At the top, off-roaders meet the road route and arrive at the highest point of the C2C – 609m. Time for a celebration! This is a fine spot on a quiet road by the 'Welcome to Northumberland – England's Border Country' sign, with moorland and hills stretching in all directions.

Watch out for the right turn just past some downhill wiggles by a couple of houses at **Paxhill**, which leads to more wiggles on a fairly easy uphill. After that, it's down, down and steeply downhill to East Allen Dale, with a tight turn followed by a road junction at the bottom that requires care. Follow the **B6295** south-east on a quiet, pleasant road through the village of **Allenheads**.

Allenheads is a small, quiet village stretched out along the East Allen Dale valley, and is home to the Allenheads Inn (*www.allenheadsinn.co.uk*), a proper old-fashioned village inn built in 1770 that extends a warm welcome to C2C riders. The inn features in the *Good Beer Guide*, serves meals and provides seven rooms for overnight accommodation with secure bike storage. The Allenheads community-owned Heritage Centre (tel: 01434 685568) next door to the inn is open most days of the year. It depicts the lead-mining history of the village, complete with Armstrong water engine and restored blacksmith's shop. Allenheads also has a village store with a post office counter, which sells confectionery, provisions, newspapers and local crafts, and the nearby Hemmel Coffee Shop serves meals and drinks daily all year in an attractive converted byre.

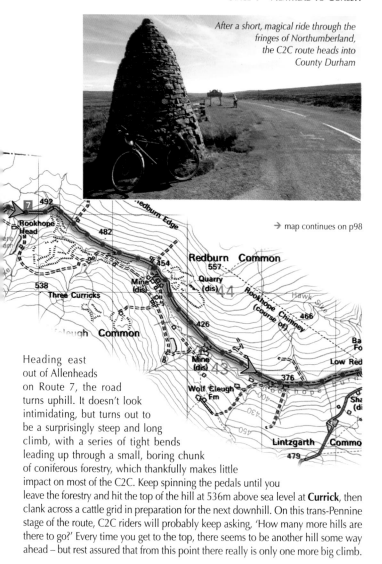

After a short, magical ride through the fringes of Northumberland, the C2C route heads into County Durham

→ map continues on p98

Heading east out of Allenheads on Route 7, the road turns uphill. It doesn't look intimidating, but turns out to be a surprisingly steep and long climb, with a series of tight bends leading up through a small, boring chunk of coniferous forestry, which thankfully makes little impact on most of the C2C. Keep spinning the pedals until you leave the forestry and hit the top of the hill at 536m above sea level at **Currick**, then clank across a cattle grid in preparation for the next downhill. On this trans-Pennine stage of the route, C2C riders will probably keep asking, 'How many more hills are there to go?' Every time you get to the top, there seems to be another hill some way ahead – but rest assured that from this point there really is only one more big climb.

95

But first, the downhill towards Rookhope is absolutely magnificent – perhaps the most enjoyable downhill ride of the entire C2C. It's long and steady with just the right gradient to coast downhill at speed or add occasional turbo-boost by twirling the pedals in the lowest gear. Apart from extensive moorland scenery, there are fine industrial relics by the side of the road. The C2C route rushes past the old fluorspar pithead at **Grove Rake Mine**, which was worked by Weardale Minerals until the late 20th century, and passes close by the splendid Lintzgarth Arch, once part of a 3km (2 mile) horizontal 'chimney' that allowed poisonous gases from Rookhope's lead-smelting works to escape on the high moors.

All too soon that memorable downhill is over and you enter the former lead and fluorspar village of **Rookhope**.

Rookhope offers refreshment and accommodation. The Rookhope Inn (*www.rookhope.com*) is directly on the C2C route, just by the track leading to the off-road route across Stanhope Common. This *Good Beer Guide* pub is owned and run by the local community, serving drinks and meals every day and offering B&B with five double rooms in a pleasant location. There are several other B&Bs in and around the village.

Ride through Rookhope until the road bears left past the Rookhope Inn. Just opposite the pub discover a lovely miniature public garden with two benches, which is

Pause to enjoy the delightful gardens at Rookhope, which provide a perfect place for a short break

Climb to the top of Boltslaw Incline and savour the view westwards – in clear weather probably the finest on the C2C

a lovely spot to sit down and take a break on a sunny day. It's also right next to the turn-off along **Hylton Terrace** for the route across Stanhope Common, the longest off-road section of the C2C (described below).

There's just one catch to the off-road route. Access to a large chunk of this wild ride has been granted by the Stanhope Syndicate, which manages grouse shooting on the heather-covered moorland. This means that after 'the glorious 12th' of August the route may be closed during the shooting season, which ends in early December. This is indicated by a sign at the start of the route but closure dates are not publicised in advance.

If the off-road route is closed, follow the **alternative road route** into Stanhope, a pleasant enough ride to an interesting small town with a cobbled market place, built on the banks of the River Wear. Follow the road round to the right through to **Rookhope** and continue towards Stanhope. The C2C route follows the side of the A689 into **Stanhope**, from where the B6278 leads uphill towards **Parkhead Station**, close to the end of the off-road route across Stanhope Common. The 7 mile road route is certainly a lot quicker than the shorter off-road option. But the main disadvantage of the road route is that it involves cycling from Stanhope to Parkhead for about 3km (2 miles) on the B6278, which combines a steep uphill grunt with the likelihood of more traffic than you have become accustomed to on the C2C.

Roadies and those who want to finish the C2C as quickly as possible should opt for the road route via Stanhope. Anyone else should try the off-road route if the weather is decent. It is a unique experience!

For the **off-road route** follow the track quite steeply uphill out of Rookhope – it will be a push if you don't have a mountain bike. It's easy to follow, with the gradient getting easier and the track surface improving as it heads up the **Boltslaw Incline** to the final high point on the eastern side of the C2C. In the 19th century, this was the site of a standing steam engine used to pull carriages piled high with iron ore and limestone up rails on the long incline, which is now a

alternative on-road route via Stanhope

simple track. The track heads up through a deep cutting. In fine weather, this is a magnificent place to stop for a picnic, with superb views across the Pennines to the west. Cyclists can also savour the thought that all the hard climbing is finished – from the top of **Bolts Law** it's downhill to Sunderland or Tynemouth virtually all the way.

At the top of the incline, pass the ruined buildings where the standing engine was located, with the crumbling stonework thankfully recently restored. From here ride across the middle of the grouse moor on a good track, passing the 'butts' (hopefully without any

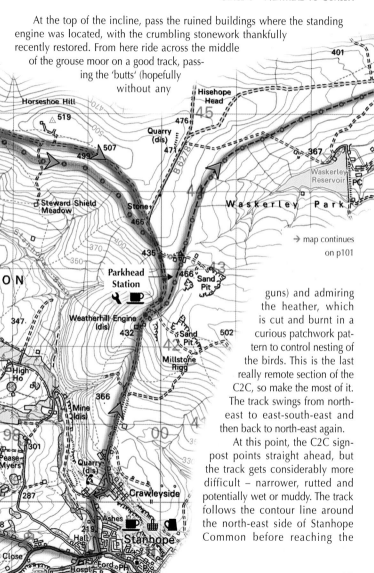

→ map continues on p101

guns) and admiring the heather, which is cut and burnt in a curious patchwork pattern to control nesting of the birds. This is the last really remote section of the C2C, so make the most of it. The track swings from north-east to east-south-east and then back to north-east again.

At this point, the C2C sign-post points straight ahead, but the track gets considerably more difficult – narrower, rutted and potentially wet or muddy. The track follows the contour line around the north-east side of Stanhope Common before reaching the

B6278 opposite an unsurfaced lane leading to Parkhead Station, where it rejoins the road route.

Following the track is fine if you enjoy mildly technical riding on a mountain bike, but riders with hybrids may find it a lot easier to follow the main track that bears left on a slight uphill, where it becomes rough and bumpy but soon brings you to the road at the splendidly named **Dead Friar's Stone**. This provides an **alternative road route** along **Meadows Edge**, running parallel to the last part of the C2C off-road route between Edmonbyers and Stanhope Common. This road should be pretty quiet, with the benefit of fine views all around, but watch for fast traffic at the **B6278** junction, close to where the off-road route joins the road. From there, it's a short roll downhill to the turn-off for Parkhead Station, pleasantly situated at the western end of the Waskerley Way.

> **Parkhead Station** is the former station master's house, now a tea room and B&B, which provides a break from the C2C in a delightful off-road setting at the start of the Waskerley Way. The fully licensed tea rooms are open all year, serving home-made food and sandwiches. B&B options include the use of two double or two family rooms with evening meals, secure cycle storage and drying room for wet gear. Parkhead Station sells cycling maps and brochures, arranges bike hire and are can provide basic tools and spares.
>
> **More information** *www.parkheadstation.co.uk*

Having crossed Stanhope Common, you can't miss the turn-off for Parkhead Station

The **Waskerley Way** follows the route of the former Stanhope and Tyne Railway, which hauled limestone and coal between Stanhope and Tyne Dock in South Shields. It provides a supremely easy and enjoyable cycle ride all the way to Lydgetts Junction on the outskirts of Consett, following traffic-free tracks with surfaces ranging from tarmac to cinder, 95 per cent of which should be good for hybrids in virtually any weather (although, as always, beware of skidding on loose gravel). The first section provides open views towards Waskerley Reservoir, which looks inviting in the midst of Waskerley Park, then the route gradually leaves wild moorland behind as it leads into tamer countryside, steadily becoming more urbanised without reducing the enjoyment of riding this track. There is the occasional gate to unlatch, designed to deter motorbikes, and these are also a useful reminder to slow down and give way to walkers enjoying the Waskerley Way.

Just past the village of **Waskerley**, the character of the track changes as it swings through a hairpin bend on the fringes of **Park Head Plantation**, joining a short narrow section that is fine when dry but better suited to mountain bikes in wet weather. Look out for the signpost to Bee Cottage (www.bee-cottage.co.uk), just a few minutes off the C2C route. This isolated guesthouse provides B&B plus dinner in a comfortable environment, with secure cycle storage and drying facilities. It could be a useful place for your last night's accommodation, approximately 48km (30 miles) from the end of the C2C.

→ map continues on p102

The Waskerley Way continues towards Consett, with a carefully designed junction helping to ensure a safe crossing of the A68 – after more than 160km (100 miles) of cycling, it may be very difficult to understand why motorised traffic needs to travel at such speed! The next highlight of the route is crossing the splendid Hownsgill Viaduct, which has stood for over 130 years and is a magnificent example of Victorian railway engineering on the course of the old Stanhope & Tyne Railway. Unfortunately, The Samaritans' phone number has to be posted at both ends and in the middle of this very high bridge.

Hownsgill Viaduct is 53m high, with neither a river nor stream beneath, just a dry valley or wind gap. This was an extreme handicap for the railway, and before the viaduct's construction freight wagons had to be lowered and raised on inclines by a stationary steam engine in order to cross the ravine. The viaduct was built during 1857–8 under the direction of Thomas Bouch and required almost 3 million white firebricks, weighing approximately 12,000 tonnes. It is 213m long, 53m high and has 12 arches, each with a 15m span. Thomas Bouch became even more famous when he built the Tay Bridge – but then became infamous when it fell down!

Hownsgill Bunkhouse and Tea-Room (*www.c2cstopoff. co.uk*) at nearby Hownsgill Farm provides self-catering accommodation in a former milking parlour on a working farm, and its location makes it well suited as a base for the eastern part of the C2C.

A wonderful red railway relic turns out to be a smelt wagon parked at **Lydgetts Junction**, indicating that the route is getting close to Consett. At this point, there is a decision to be made as to which of the two alternative routes to take to the

Ride across the superb Hownsgill Viaduct on the final approach to Consett

end of the C2C. For the route that finishes at Sunderland, continue straight ahead on the Consett & Sunderland Railway Path (see Stage 5a). Cyclists wishing to finish at Tynemouth (see Stage 5b) should either turn off here on Route 14 towards Gateshead and South Shields or, for an alternative start to this stage, continue past Terris Novalis to the A692 roundabout at Templeton, and follow a sign to Newcastle and Tynemouth to join with the main Stage 5b route.

CONSETT

Until 1840, 'Conside' was a tiny hamlet on the eastern bank of the River Derwent, its name derived from the Old English word for 'side of a hilltop'. Little more than a year later, the Derwent Iron Company had transformed Conside into the iron and steel powerhouse of Consett, boosting the population from under 200 to over 5000 people.

By 1875 the Derwent Iron Company was the largest producer of iron plates used in the Tyne and Wear shipyards and a major supplier to the booming railway industry. Consett steel became famous throughout the world, but eventually lost its economic viability due to competition from India and other new steel nations. The huge steelworks finally closed on 12 Sept 1980. Today, nothing remains apart from sculptural artefacts such as the two red smelt wagons at Lydgetts Junction.

STAGE 5A

CONSETT TO SUNDERLAND

Distance	40km (25 miles)
Time	2–3hrs
Ascent	253m
Descent	504m
Start	Car park at Lydgetts Junction, Consett, GR495098

One of two alternative routes to finish the C2C – either at Sunderland or Tynemouth. This option is quicker and easier to navigate, but less inspirational than the route to Newcastle. It's all downhill to the finish by Roker Pier in Sunderland, but there is plenty to see and do along the route. It is a good idea to leave plenty of time to enjoy this last stage of the C2C, particularly if you plan to visit the Beamish Open Air Museum or Washington Wildfowl and Wetlands Centre.

At the north-eastern end of the Waskerley Way, the C2C route joins the start of the Consett & Sunderland Railway Path, close to a car park by the smelt wagons at **Lydgetts Junction**. It continues straight ahead, passing the **Terris Novalis** sculptures before arriving on the outskirts of Consett by the A692 roundabout at **Templetown**. Here look out for a rather splendid, black cast iron signpost with arms like a bird that points the way to Tynemouth or Sunderland via Stanley.

The route to Sunderland follows the southern fringes of Consett and is generally easy to follow and hassle-free, using tracks, parks and occasional stretches

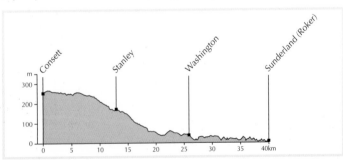

CONSETT AND SUNDERLAND SCULPTURE TRAIL

Tony Cragg designed two stainless steel artworks, known as the Terris Novalis sculptures, one a theodolite and the other an engineer's level, for the site of the old Consett steelworks. His design is inspired by the industrial past, but both sculptures have 'animal' feet, suggesting a timely return to nature, with the former steelworks restored to rolling pasture and woodland.

Old lime kilns provide an interesting diversion by the side of the railway path

Terris Novalis is the start of the Consett and Sunderland Sculpture Trail, which follows the Consett & Sunderland Railway Path from Consett to Chester Le Street and is extremely varied. Banks of earth are piled up to form an extraordinary section of 'waves' on the outskirts of Leadgate, transforming the cycle path into a miniature slalom course. This is the 'Jolly Drovers Maze', originally created by Andy Goldsworthy in 1989 on the site of the former Eden Pit Colliery. Two huge and forbidding steel 'men' – 'The Old Transformers' by David Kemp – gaze across a particularly attractive section of the path below Pontop Pike, as you ride quickly beneath. Other sculptures are more modest, with simple steel shields pointing to disused lime kilns by the side of the old railway and four steel cows near the Beamish Museum.

of quiet road to break free of the town. Follow the signpost across the **Templetown roundabout** and join a narrow cycle path/walkway, with clear C2C signposting, through a park to a fairly busy road crossing, which is not helped by traffic belting round a blind bend. Cross carefully and bear left to follow a tarmac cycle path, keeping an open expanse of pleasant parkland on your right.

→ map continues on p106

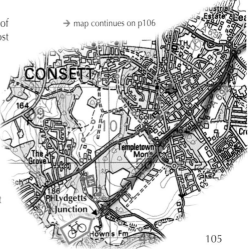

You are being watched!
Riding beneath 'The Old Transformers',
one of the highlights of the sculpture trail

The C2C continues to provide good traffic-free riding alongside the **A692** in a north-easterly direction, then crosses another roundabout and follows a series of cycle paths and pavements through the suburb of **Leadgate**. At last, the cycle path reaches the **Jolly Drovers** pub at the A692 Ebchester

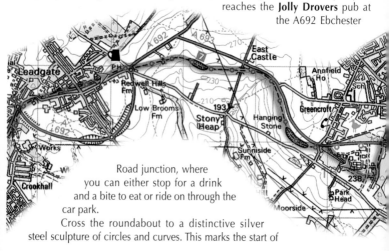

Road junction, where you can either stop for a drink and a bite to eat or ride on through the car park.

Cross the roundabout to a distinctive silver steel sculpture of circles and curves. This marks the start of

106

enjoyable riding along the **Consett & Sunderland Railway Path**, with good unsealed and tarmac surfaces for much of the remaining distance to Sunderland. After a steady climb to the **Hanging Stone** on Annfield Plain at 256m, it's downhill all the way to Sunderland apart from a couple of short climbs up the north bank of the River Wear, near Washington and Hylton Bridge (A19).

The route follows the Consett & Sunderland Railway Path past the conurbation of **Stanley**, which you hardly notice, riding briskly along the rather splendid tree-lined track beneath a succession of bridges. Between Stanley and Beamish you will pass the intriguingly named **Hellhole Wood** (managed by the Woodland Trust and part of the Great North Community Forest, with a growing population of red squirrels) before reaching the clearly signposted turn-off for Beamish Open Air Museum.

→ map continues on p108

The **Beamish Open Air Museum** tells the story of life in north-east England in Georgian, Victorian and Edwardian times, set in 300 acres of beautiful County Durham countryside. Most of the houses, shops and other buildings are original to the area, and have been brought to Beamish, rebuilt and furnished as they once were. Some, such as Home Farm, Pockerley Old Hall and the drift mine were already there. Allow at least half a day for a visit. Tickets are quite expensive, but there is a great deal to see and do, plus the opportunity for free visits during the rest of the year.

More information *www.beamish.org.uk*

One downside of the Consett & Sunderland Railway Path is having to negotiate a succession of barriers and gates designed to keep out motor-bikers, which can be a little frustrating if you are in a rush to reach Sunderland. One solution is to relax and enjoy yourself – what's the hurry? From a more practical perspective, Sustrans are working towards making the C2C more accessible to disabled riders wherever they can and to that end have recently removed the central hoops. The railway path crosses the modern **railway line** just north of Chester Le Street, then crosses over the top of the **A1**, successfully sticking to a green route on the outskirts of **Washington**, a large urban splurge sandwiched between Gateshead and Sunderland.

It is a pleasant change of scenery when the C2C route turns downhill through James Steel Park to follow the west bank of the **River Wear**. If it's time for a beer, cross the footbridge to the Oddfellows Arms on the opposite bank. If not, follow the C2C route along a quiet lane on a short and unexpectedly steep uphill, joining the side of a road by the municipal sewage works where a cycle path leads directly past the main entrance of the **Washington's Wildfowl and Wetlands Trust Centre**.

Wildfowl and Wetlands Trust (WWT) is a leading conservation organisation saving wetlands for wildlife and people across the world. It is also the only UK charity with a national network of specialist wetland visitor centres, including the **Washington Wetlands Centre**. Its varied landscape of wetlands, meadows and woodlands is a haven for overwintering migratory water birds, and has large flocks of curlews and redshanks – you may see ducks, geese, waders, flamingos, cranes, herons, frogs, bats and even goats!

More information www.wwt.org.uk

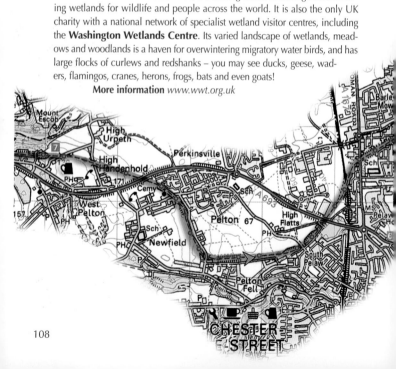

The C2C's final approach to Sunderland runs alongside the busy **A1231** road, so don't expect peace and quiet. But do not despair, as the last few miles of the route follow a superb cycle path on the **River Wear Trail**, where the road is out of sight and out of mind. This provides a tranquil and beautiful finish to the C2C, with interesting Heritage Information Paving Stones to ponder over and architectural relics to admire.

→ map continues on p110

Cycle on beneath the superb **Queen Victoria Viaduct**, completed on the day of the queen's coronation in 1838, passing a witty sign that tells C2C riders to 'Keep Going!' Ride past the National Glass Centre where you can look at 1300 years of glass making on Wearside, next to the ultra-modern University of Sunderland in a superb riverside location beside a giant

Cycle under the Queen Victoria Viaduct, finished on the day of the queen's coronation and still in use

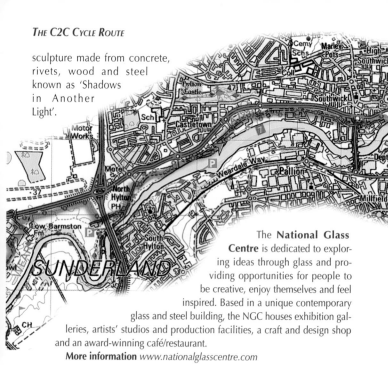

sculpture made from concrete, rivets, wood and steel known as 'Shadows in Another Light'.

The **National Glass Centre** is dedicated to exploring ideas through glass and providing opportunities for people to be creative, enjoy themselves and feel inspired. Based in a unique contemporary glass and steel building, the NGC houses exhibition galleries, artists' studios and production facilities, a craft and design shop and an award-winning café/restaurant.

More information *www.nationalglasscentre.com*

The C2C ends with a superb ride along a new cycle path that follows the north bank of the River Wear towards the North Sea

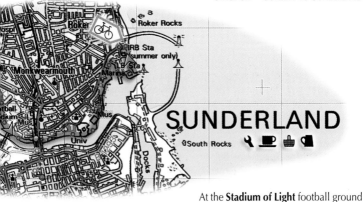

At the **Stadium of Light** football ground there are two route options – one via the river's edge and the other via the stadium entrance, which also offers the option to cycle into the city centre with a link route to the railway station.

Keep cycling past **Sunderland harbour** and around the side of the **yacht marina**, passing the lifeboat station and then turning left to head north along the promenade towards Roker's long curving pier. A little further on, pass an Inshore Lifeboat Station on the **Roker** seafront – a pleasant suburb of Sunderland – and be ready to enjoy a peephole view through 'C', a large granite monolith designed by artist Andrew Small to frame **Roker Lighthouse** and celebrate the end of the C2C. Next to it is a black granite noticeboard erected by Sunderland City Council displaying rather more fundamental information on the C2C, and which rather touchingly suggests 'Come back soon!' It's a bit of an anti-climax, but very

The C2C finish line is perfectly aligned with the lighthouse on the end of Roker Pier

111

The finish – 134 miles from Whitehaven!

nice to arrive! As a well-deserved bonus, there's a good choice of pubs, cafés and restaurants nearby.

If you don't have time to join another cycle route (see 'Getting There and Getting Back' in the Introduction), but need to get straight home, there is a signed cycle route to Sunderland station (3km/2 miles away) from the finish.

TWO RIVERS CYCLEWAY

What happens when you get to the finish of the C2C at Roker near Sunderland? You could continue along the Two Rivers Cycleway, following NCN Route 1 for 13km (8 miles) along the coast to South Shields. From South Shields, it's possible to follow Route 14 westwards along the south side of the River Tyne, with options of crossing on the ferry to North Shields, cycling under the river on the Tyne pedestrian and cycle tunnel from Jarrow, or crossing to Newcastle's glamorous riverside on the Gateshead Millennium Bridge.

STAGE 5B

CONSETT TO TYNEMOUTH

Distance	43km (27 miles)
Time	3–5hrs
Ascent	353m
Descent	577m
Start	Car park at Lydgetts Junction, Consett, GR495098

This alternative finish to the C2C initially follows the Derwent Walk along a superb railway path for most of the distance to the River Tyne. The next section includes a fine ride along the waterfront at Newcastle upon Tyne, before the C2C heads towards Tynemouth and the North Sea.

→ map continues on p114

On the approach to Consett, cyclists can choose either of two ways to access the Derwent Walk railway path, bound for Newcastle and Tynemouth. The two routes join up on the west side of Blackhill and Consett Park. First – on the Waskerley Way, 1.5km (1 mile) to the south-west of Consett, Route 14 crosses Route 7 at **Lydgetts Junction**, close to a red smelt wagon. The route joins a track behind a car park that bears north to cross the **A692**. Follow Derwent Walk signs to the outskirts of Consett, where the C2C follows roads through **Blackhill** to join the Derwent Walk just before crossing the **A691**.

The second option – ride past **Terris Novalis** on the Consett & Sunderland Railway Path and arrive by the side of the A692 roundabout at **Templeton**. A large black C2C signpost with arms like a bird points three ways to Durham and Allenheads, Leadgate and Stanley, Newcastle and Tynemouth, the last being the way to go.

113

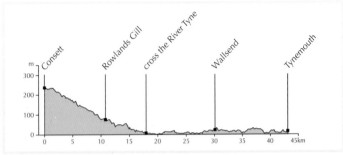

Cycle along the pavement (strictly legal) to the left, passing a clutch of fast-food outlets and drive-through superstores on the opposite side of the road.

→ map continues on p116

There is a clear sign to cross over into Blackhill and Consett Park, which was laid out on reclaimed land by the Consett Iron Company and gifted to the community in 1891. Initially, there is a choice of tarmac paths across rolling parkland and C2C signposting becomes rather vague. The correct route is to keep to the left side of the hill, decorated with a few fine industrial relics from the steelworks that covered this whole area. But if you go straight over the hill it makes no odds – just turn left when you reach the next road, then turn right into the splendour of the formal gardens of **Blackhill and Consett Park**, where it may be pleasant to stop and admire the excellent flower beds from one of many benches. Ride on down past the splendid bandstand, cross the

If you have followed NCN7 all the way to the Templeton roundabout on the outskirts of Consett, take the left signpost for Rowlands Gill and Newcastle

road with care by the church and go straight ahead on **St Aidans Street** to link with Route 14 on the C2C.

Turn right from St Aidans Street through a peaceful housing estate, with lawns and trees, following the route indicated by the black-winged steel signpost pointing towards Shotley Bridge and Rowlands Gill. Cross the next road and go straight ahead to join the **Derwent Walk**, possibly the most enjoyable cycle path on the entire C2C route.

> The **Derwent Walk** follows the former Derwent Valley railway line for 16km (10 miles) between Swalwell and Consett. It was converted into a path for walkers and bridleway for horse-riders and cyclists after the last train ran in 1963. It is delightful for many reasons, not least because it's a slight but steady downhill all the way. Much of the path passes through beautiful woodland, with the trees forming a canopy, and on a sunny day it's like riding through a glittering tunnel. When the trees open out there are some great views. The track itself is fairly wide and has a good cinder surface for a smooth, quiet ride, and the path leads across some superb bridges and viaducts. Lastly, it always seems reasonably litter-free, probably because it successfully avoids built-up areas.

Follow the Derwent Walk past **Ebchester**, close to the Vindomora Roman Fort, where there's an information board next to a pleasant spot with fine views over

115

The former Derwent Valley railway line is now a superb cycle route to Rowlands Gill.

neighbouring hills and picnic tables. The path crosses the River Derwent on a superb bridge just before **Rowlands Gill**, where the railway path is temporarily interrupted by roads. Follow well-marked cycle paths along the side of the **B6314** and **A694**, passing a garage before turning right onto the continuation of the Derwent Walk. This diversion should take no more than 5mins. Look out for the Column to

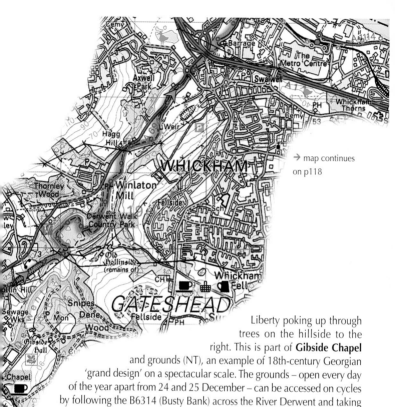

→ map continues
on p118

Liberty poking up through trees on the hillside to the right. This is part of **Gibside Chapel** and grounds (NT), an example of 18th-century Georgian 'grand design' on a spectacular scale. The grounds – open every day of the year apart from 24 and 25 December – can be accessed on cycles by following the B6314 (Busty Bank) across the River Derwent and taking the first left turn.

The Derwent Walk crosses the 152m-long **Nine Arches Viaduct**, a superb bridge overlooking the Derwent Valley, built for the simple reason that the Earl of Strathmore would not allow the railway to pass through his Gibside Estate. Having crossed the viaduct, the C2C turns left off the Derwent Walk railway path to continue through **Derwenthaugh Park** in extremely attractive surroundings, with ornamental lakes and landscaped grounds replacing the former coke works on the north bank of the River Derwent. Ride carefully through the park, which is popular with local walkers, pram pushers, cyclists and motorised scooters for the disabled.

The C2C route leaves the park to follow the side of the river on traffic-free cycle paths that eventually run alongside the **A694** and then pass underneath the **A1** and **A1114** on the outskirts of **Gateshead** as the Derwent flows into much larger River Tyne. At this point, take care with navigation. Keelmans Way (C2C

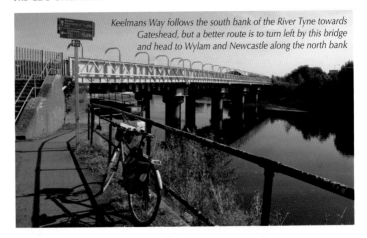

Keelmans Way follows the south bank of the River Tyne towards Gateshead, but a better route is to turn left by this bridge and head to Wylam and Newcastle along the north bank

Route 14) follows the south side of the River Tyne but is not particularly enjoyable, so Wylam and Newcastle (Route 72) is a better way to go. It doesn't seem logical to start cycling upriver away from Newcastle, but this route crosses the River Tyne by the **A695 road bridge**, which has a shared-use footway for walkers and cyclists. On the north bank, a dedicated bridge for walkers and cyclists makes crossing the busy A695 relatively stress-free, tempered by occasional small motorbikes using the same facility.

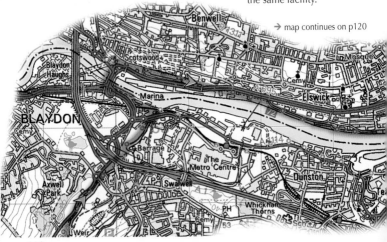

→ map continues on p120

The C2C now shares Route 72 with Hadrian's Cycleway and parts of Hadrian's long-distance footpath. After a brief pedal through parkland, the route follows a shared-use pavement along both sides of the busy **A695** – the pavement provides safe cycling that is reasonably stress-free. But it's a great relief when Route 72 turns away from the road and heads down towards the river at **Elswick**, starting a delightful traffic-free section that goes right into middle of Newcastle. Stop to read all the information boards to learn fascinating snippets from the industrial and shipping heritage of the River Tyne. Marvel at the wonderful series of bridges that connect Gateshead to Newcastle as you cycle beneath them.

TYNESIDE BRIDGES ON THE C2C

Newcastle's wonderful bridges make cycling along the waterfront a memorable experience

- **King Edward VII Bridge**, built in 1902–06 for the North Eastern Railway Company in steel on stone piers
- **Metro Bridge**, built 1976–80 for Metro trains in steel-truss construction
- **High Level Bridge**, the oldest and highest bridge of them all, built as a double-deck stone and steel structure 1846–9; reopened 2008 after a £43 million restoration
- **Swing Bridge**, steel bridge built 1868–76 with electric hydraulic swinging mechanism to allow shipping to go upstream
- **Tyne Bridge**, the biggest single-span bridge in Britain when opened by King George V in 1928; built as a steel arch 1925–8
- **Gateshead Millennium Bridge** (above), pedestrian and cycle bridge forming a huge arc across the river; tilting, steel, electrically operated; built 1998–2001 from a short-list of six winning designs

There are pubs, cafés and restaurants on the river-front in the centre of **Newcastle**, or plenty of delightful benches if you prefer to enjoy an al fresco picnic. These days Newcastle's riverside feels like a smart Mediterranean resort!

Cyclists might expect the last 16km (10 miles) of the C2C to continue along the side of the River Tyne to the finish by Tynemouth Castle. Not a bit of it! A few hundred metres past the **Millennium Bridge**, the route bears left away from the river and, apart from occasional glimpses, isn't seen again until Tynemouth. This part of the route – following Hadrian's Cycleway – is a bit higgledy-piggledy. It seems to dart all over the place, while trying to stay as traffic-free and cycle-friendly as possible, so it is as well that Route 72 signposting is excellent in both eastward and westward directions. Some riders may choose to finish their C2C at Newcastle and leave out this last section, which is not the most interesting part of the route.

The first part follows reasonably quiet roads to a cycle path at **St Lawrence**, which leads towards a pleasant ride through **Riverside Park** by St Anthony's Point, where the River Tyne turns northwards. As befits Hadrian's Cycleway, the cycle path goes right past **Segedunum Roman Fort** on the outskirts of **Wallsend**, then follows the side of Hadrian Road (A187) before swooping downhill through a park beneath the splendid **Willington Viaduct**, designed by Benjamin Green in 1838 to carry the Newcastle and North Shields Railway across Willington Gut and now used by Metro trains. The route continues to **Willington Quay**, where it crosses over the busy **A19** and **Howden by-pass**.

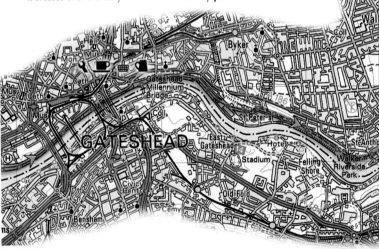

Segedunum Roman Fort stood on the banks of the River Tyne, the eastern outpost of Hadrian's Wall, which the Emperor Hadrian ordered to be built in AD122 to defend the Roman Empire from the barbarians of the north. Segedunum had a garrison of 600 soldiers for almost 300 years. The newly opened 'Roman experience' has become one of the leading attractions along the wall, with facilities including shop and café.

More information *www.twmuseums.org.uk*

→ map continues on p122

This leads to a pleasant pedal through a sculpture park to **Royal Quays Marina**, where the route temporarily rejoins the River Tyne by **Shields harbour**. Follow the C2C signposts round the edge of the marina, then away from the river through **North Shields** until the route drops down by the river at **Union Quay**, where there are fish shops and restaurants in an attractive location on a sunny day – the perfect excuse for a final slap-up lunch on the C2C!

Union Quay is an excellent place to stop if you enjoy freshly cooked fish

121

The route continues to wiggle and wind towards the finish near Tynemouth Castle. Ride out onto the waterfront, looking through the River Tyne entrance between the **North** and **South piers** for a first view of the North Sea. The two long piers were built between 1854 and 1895, but the North Pier was partially destroyed by a storm in 1887 and restored only in 1909. Follow the left wing of the red steel signpost as you pedal round the promenade on the last few hundred metres of the C2C, passing beneath **Collingwood's Monument**, an imposing statue and plinth erected by public subscription in 1845 to the memory of Admiral Lord Collingwood, who led the British fleet into action at Trafalgar on 21 Oct 1805. The **finish sign** is appropriately on a hillock, also indicating the start of Hadrian's Cycleway (NCN Route 72), the Reivers Route (NCN Route 10) and Coast & Castles (NCN Route 1). It's a lovely spot to savour your success on a fine afternoon, but not a good place to hang around when a gale is blowing off the North Sea!

The finish at Tynemouth

WHERE NEXT?

Take a short walk up the hill, enjoy the view of the castle and priory, then work out how to get home!

- If you wish to visit Tynemouth Castle and Priory, push your bike up and over the hill.
- Don't make the mistake of riding to the nearby Metro station, for a quick trip back to Newcastle's main railway station, unless you have a folding bike (bikes aren't allowed on the trains).
- The best option is to cycle back to Newcastle for a train. From the Millennium Bridge waterfront, allow at least 15mins to find Newcastle's main station, which is steeply uphill on non cycle-friendly roads – you may find it easier to push your bike along the wide pavements.

A fine steel signpost indicates the route through Cumbria University campus, linking Keswick with Penrith and Sunderland on the C2C (Route 5)

TASTER ROUTES

ROUTE 1

LAKELAND LOOP	
Distance	25.5km (16 miles) (+ 6.5km/4 miles for visit to Cockermouth; + 16km/10 miles if starting/finishing at Keswick)
Start/finish	Parking area at Powter How, near the old Swan Hotel, on minor road parallel to the A66 at the southern end of Bassenthwaite Lake (GR 221265)
Map	Explorer OL4

An enjoyable circuit on the west side of the Lake District, using sections of C2C Stages 1a and 1b, which is not too challenging. The route provides plenty of riding on woodland tracks, some wonderful views and the option of visiting the fine old market town of Cockermouth. It is also possible to start from Keswick, which adds an extra 8km (5 miles) each way.

From Powter How ride south along the old road to arrive at the three-way C2C signpost on the right. Turn sharp right to follow the Whitehaven direction, but watch carefully for the sharp left turn up through the woods. From here it's a long, steady ride uphill through Whinlatter Forest, following tracks that are sometimes quite steep (at other times not so bad), but always easy to follow, with a good surface for any bike with reasonably fat tyres. There are two lovely picnic spots to break the climb – by a small lake with waterfalls and at a clearing with fine easterly views towards the fells.

Watch out for other cyclists coming downhill. The forest park is popular with riders having a day in the woods, although hard-core cyclists are likely to use the special mountain-bike track. Ride out past the visitor centre and through the car park, then turn downhill on the road. But not too far or fast – the next right turn comes up quickly, and here follow the C2C sign into the south side of Whinlatter Forest Park. Follow the track through the woods on a fairly easy undulating trail, then join the road in magnificent surroundings by Hobcarton Gill.

After a few hundred metres on the B5292, which is a quiet road, follow the C2C route as it bears left on an up-and-down narrow lane that soon plunges downhill, with magnificent views to the west out over the Solway Firth and Irish Sea. This is a tough uphill in the other direction, but steady and very pleasant

Looking downhill as the Lakeland Loop heads west towards High Lorton

on the way down. One of the finest hills on the C2C, it has superb views, lovely surroundings, is not too much of a struggle going up and is not too hairy going down – plus there's a bench at the halfway stage which is perfect for a sit down.

Ride on downhill past Scales Farm into High Lorton at the foot of the fells. There's a small general store with a weatherboard front for provisions, as well as plenty of choice for B&B. This is where the Lakeland Loop leaves the C2C, which continues towards Whitehaven by turning left along the east side of the River Cocker. (When the bridge at Low Lorton is restored, the C2C will presumably revert to the west side of the River Cocker, where the route is a little more cycle-friendly.)

To continue the Lakeland Loop towards Cockermouth, turn right along the B5289 at Low Lorton. The road winds through flat terrain with high hedges, which slows down motorists and provides a gentle route for cyclists. Ride on past the junction with the B5292 leading back to High Lorton and look out for a narrow, unsignposted lane on the right. Turn into this lane and ride uphill towards a solitary house at High Armaside, then bear left with the lane as it follows the contours of the hillside.

Stay left until you ride uphill to a T-junction, turning north-east along Hundith Hill Road and joining Route 71 from Workington at the intersection of Strawberry How Road, where there is the option of paying a visit to Cockermouth (an additional 6.5km/4 miles return). Continue to follow the C2C route from Cockermouth to Bassenthwaite (as described in Section 1b) or Keswick.

ROUTE 2

WEST COAST LOOP

Distance	74km (46 miles)
Start/finish	Workington Lighthouse (GR 983297)
Maps	Explorer 303, OL4

A clockwise circuit of the western section of the C2C (Stages 1a and 1b), connecting Whitehaven and Workington on the coast with Cockermouth and the Vale of Lorton on the fringe of the Lake District National Park.

Start this ride from the C2C start/finish sign, making use of the convenient car park adjacent to Workington Lighthouse. Alternatively, start from Whitehaven or Cockermouth, both of which have plenty of car parking.

From Workington Lighthouse, follow the C2C route to Cockermouth, as described in Stage 1b. Continue on the C2C route out of Cockermouth, following Strawberry How Road across the A66. About 750m on, leave the C2C route by taking the first right turn into Hundith Hill Road. Take the next left turn downhill and follow a narrow country lane past High Armaside, then follow the lane as it turns right down towards the B5292.

The West Coast Loop heads towards Lamplugh on the western fringe of the fells

Turn left along the B5292 and follow the road south as it weaves between hedges. At the next junction, fork right onto the B5289 and take the next left turn onto a lane, which continues straight ahead towards a crossroads at Cross Gates. Here, pick up the next C2C signpost for Route 71 to Whitehaven. Continue straight ahead, following the narrow lane up and down along the hillside, while heading south on the east side of Lorton Vale. The C2C route rejoins the B5289 for a few hundred metres, then forks left on a lane leading towards Loweswater. (If Lorton Low Bridge reopens, cyclists can follow the lane on the west side of Lorton Vale, which was the former C2C route.)

Follow the C2C route along the north-east side of Loweswater. The roads here are very quiet, but be prepared for some short, sharp uphills as the route leave the lakes behind and follows the route up to Fangs Brow Farm. Turn left here and admire fine views of rolling fells before tackling a relentless but steady climb through Lamplugh and Kirkland. (After that there's one more climb before it's all downhill towards the sea beyond Whitehaven.) In clear weather there are fine views all around, so make the most of them before leaving the road by the school-house between Kirkland and Rowrah and joining a winding track between old quarries, which leads onto the tarmac railway path.

Then enjoy 13km (8 miles) of easy riding on a traffic-free, gentle downhill, before the ride through Whitehaven brings you down to earth. The C2C is well signposted, but follows a tortuous route through sombre suburbs in order to avoid traffic, although this becomes unavoidable on the last leg to the harbour, where the C2C start/finish pillar is found down by the water. To complete the West Coast Loop, follow the Whitehaven to Workington link (described after Stage 1b).

ROUTE 3

WESTERN C2C LOOP

Distance	88.5km (55 miles) (+ 16km/10 miles for start/finish at Keswick)
Route	Whitehaven – Workington – Cockermouth – Wythop Woods (Bassenthwaite Lake) – Whinlatter Forest – Whinlatter Pass – Lorton – Loweswater – Lamplugh – Whitehaven
Maps	Explorer 303, OL4

Combine the Lakeland Loop and West Coast Loop for a big circuit of the western part of the C2C, with the option of starting and finishing at Keswick or anywhere convenient on the circuit.

ROUTE 4

THE OLD COACH ROAD

Distance	55km (34 miles)
Start/finish	Greystoke (GR 441309)
Maps	Explorer OL4, OL5

This clockwise circuit combines the C2C on- and off-road routes between Keswick and Greystoke (C2C Stage 2), including the Old Coach Road, which provides a superb off-road experience. If you're not in a hurry, allow a full day to enjoy this ride.

This ride starts and finishes at Greystoke, where there is a car park on the Penrith road. Alternatively, cyclists can start and finish at Keswick – or anywhere convenient along the route. The big attraction is the Old Coach Road, which runs through wild country above Threlkeld Common. It's a rough ride perfectly suited to mountain bikes, but is also enjoyable on a good hybrid or touring bike – you will just need to push on some of the more demanding sections. It is best tackled on a clear, dry day, when you can make the most of magnificent views amid wild nature. (If it's raining, it is advisable to keep off the Old Coach Road.)

Follow the road heading south out of Greystoke towards Motherby, passing the Boot and Shoe pub and 13th-century church. Some 750m from the village, turn off on the first lane to the left, signposted towards Greystoke Gill, with a reassuring blue C2C sign for Route 71. Stay right at the next junction and follow this quiet country road up and down to the A66. Cross this fast road with care, then pause to admire superb views of rolling green countryside framed by high Lakeland hills.

All part of the fun – crossing the narrow bridge at Thornsgill Beck

Follow the spider's web of delightful country lanes through Hutton John, Sparkes Mill, Thackthwaite and Nabend to the B5288. Route 71 is clearly signposted, but be prepared for some stiff, short climbs. The route continues south past Brownrigg Farm, after which bear right along Matterdale Rigg towards the A5091 at Matterdale End.

129

Riding surfaces on the Old Coach Road are best suited to mountain bikes, but on a sturdy hybrid you'll only need to push over short sections

Cross straight over the A5091 and ride up a track on the corner, which winds steeply uphill past a few houses, joining a bridleway on a good level surface that leads westwards to New Road on the edge of forestry below Pencil Crag. Turn left along New Road and follow it south past a forestry plantation on Cockley Moor, then swoop downhill towards a small car-parking area by a sheepfold at High Row. This is where the C2C route joins the Old Coach Road, following the right-turn signpost for 'St John's in the Vale – Unsuitable for motor vehicles'.

On the Old Coach Road a 'Hierarchy of Trail Routes' notice has been posted by the Land Access and Recreation Association (LARA). This clearly states that the Old Coach Road is popular with cyclists, and that 4x4s and motorcycles should respect all other users, travel slowly, and be prepared to give way and switch off engines. Unfortunately, some drivers do not always abide by these guidelines.

Cyclists on hybrid bikes will find that they cope with the rough track, in spite of puddles and some rock-strewn downhills. Mountain bikes would certainly be faster, but the principal reason to follow the Old Coach Road is surely to take time to enjoy the superb views and make a much stronger connection with the wild Lakeland fells than is possible on the main route of the C2C.

The Old Coach Road starts fairly easily, crossing the tumbling water of Groove Beck in a delightful landscape beneath High Brow. The track continues along Barbary Rigg and Mothersike Brow, where the surface breaks up and riding gets more difficult as the track progresses westwards – which isn't so bad when you can enjoy wonderful views across Threlkeld Common to mighty Blencathra, one of the Lake District's highest fells, with Keswick coming into sight down the valley. The Old Coach Road ends with a long downhill from Hausewell Brow on a rough, loose surface that would make this a 'technical' descent for mountain bikers. This would be a tough climb in the opposite direction, making it preferable to ride the Old Coach Road from east to west.

Ride out onto the lane at the end of the Old Coach Road, where C2C 71 signposts the way to Keswick via Castlerigg or the railway path. If you are interested in prehistory, the stone circle at Castlerigg is well worth a visit. Turn right and immediately left on the road, following a narrow lane with a few easy ups and downs past Wanthwaite Mill and Shundraw to Naddle Bridge, where you take the next left turn and climb uphill to the stone circle.

Castlerigg stone circle (National Trust and English Heritage) is the most visited stone circle in Cumbria. There are 38 stones, standing up to 2.3m high, arranged in a circle approximately 30m in diameter, with a rectangle of 10 more standing stones inside the circle. It was probably built around 3000BC at the beginning of the later Neolithic period, and is considered important in terms of megalithic astronomy and geometry. Entry is free and the setting is superb, set on the level top of low hills with fine views to Skiddaw, Blencathra and Lonscale Fell.

Castlerigg Stone Circle on the outskirts of Keswick is well worth a visit and is easily accessed by bike

Be aware that most people who visit the stone circle come up by car from Keswick, so be careful on the steep, potentially fast downhill that leads towards the town. This narrow road leads to the outskirts of Keswick near Chestnut Hill, where it filters into the main road. Follow the A5271 downhill, but don't go too fast. The turn-off for the railway path comes up very quickly and is easily missed. The railway path is accessed by a narrow footpath, just before the bridge over the railway at Brigham. From here, it's a quick and easy ride to Keswick's old railway station.

You can now enjoy the delights of Keswick, with a visit to the cycle-friendly café/bike shop the Lakeland Pedlar recommended (www.lakelandpedlar.co.uk).

To continue the ride back to Greystoke, follow the main C2C route as described in Stage 2.

ROUTE 5

PENRITH TO CARLISLE

Distance	39km (24 miles) (returning by train)
Maps	OL5, 315

Route 7 provides a signposted route between Penrith (C2C Stage 2) and Carlisle (with a return by train), and is the official C2C link with the National Cycle Network in Scotland. The route makes a pleasant one-day outing, with the opportunity to explore the city of Carlisle.

There are regular train services between Penrith and Carlisle, which takes a mere 15mins. However, getting bikes on trains can be a lottery, with different policies for different train companies and only a limited number of bikes allowed, often on a first-come-first-served basis at the conductor's discretion. If you intend to travel with more than two bikes, it would certainly be wise to plan ahead or have a fall-back plan. For general information, download the 'Cycling by Train' leaflet at www.nationalrail.co.uk.

The route from Penrith to Carlisle starts with quite a few ups and downs, but not much real climbing and a general downhill trend beyond Skelton. Much of the distance is on quiet country roads, with an interesting alternative off-road route between Raughton Head and Dalton and a long traffic-free cycle path leading into the heart of Carlisle.

From Penrith, the route follows Route 7 westwards, following a farm track under the railway and M6, where it heads uphill to the Cumbria University campus at Newton Rigg. Follow the C2C signposts between the university buildings,

The alternative off-road route between Raughton Head and Dalston is a lot of fun, but only recommended in dry weather

then turn right along the road, following the steel-winged signpost in the direction of Keswick. Ride through the village of Laithes and continue to head north-west on Route 7 when the C2C (Route 71) turns left towards Little Blencow. The Carlisle route bears due north through Skelton, where there is the option of stopping for a drink at the Dog & Gun Inn, before passing a forest of radio transmitter masts that indicate the high point of the ride, with fine views of the Pennines to the east.

The route is clearly signposted towards Skelton West End, after which there are a few dips and dives, and it passes on-road and off-road turn-offs for the Reivers Cycle Route (Route 10) on the way to Raughton Head. Just past the church at Raughton Head cyclists have the choice of on- or off-road routes to Dalston. The road route briefly joins the B5299, before taking a left turn onto a minor road that heads north-west and north-east towards Dalston, where it is reunited with the off-road route. While the road route is much quicker, if it's dry, pleasant weather and you have a suitable hybrid or mountain bike, the off-road route provides a lovely ride through fine English countryside. However, it could become horribly muddy in wet weather and requires some care with navigation.

To join the off-road route, turn right onto a narrow lane past Raughton Head. This soon becomes a track heading steadily uphill. Turn left at the top and follow another track to ride across the River Caldbeck on Highwith Bridge, built of steel and planks with forestry on both sides. Follow the winding track through Willowclose Wood past an imposing country seat, which turns out to be the Lime

House School. The bridleway route continues across fine parkland, then follows a gentle downhill to a few houses at Holmhill, where the route turns right into a field by the side of a fine large house known as Hawksdale Hall. This part of the ride is lovely, with views across parkland and fields to the river, but there will be cows (and if it's wet, cows create the worst-ever mud for bikers).

There is a brief break in the off-road route at Bridge End, where navigation can appear a little confused. Follow the track (now also part of the Cumbria Way long-distance footpath) as it bends left to join the B5299. Ride downhill on this road for a short distance until it swings round a bend, with a garage and cars for sale on the bend. Almost immediately, take the next right turn right to cross the river and the route again goes off-road. (Alternatively, you may like to pause for a drink at the nearby Bridge End Inn.) The off-road route (Cumbria Way) now follows the east side of the river before emerging on the road at Dalston, where the attractive village square has a pub (Blue Bell), café (Country Kitchen) and imposing church (St Michael's) to satisfy your requirements.

On the outskirts of Dalston, the route joins a superb cycle path that provides 8km (5 miles) of traffic-free cycling on tarmac to Carlisle. It follows the River Caldbeck in surprisingly beautiful surroundings, with masses of wild flowers in summertime. You can expect to meet lots of dog walkers and locals on bikes here. On the outskirts of Carlisle, the cycle path passes an impressive weir as it leads

A delightful, immaculate tarmac cycle path follows the course of the River Caldew downstream between Dalston and Carlisle

almost to the centre of the town. Signposting for cyclists is excellent, with a short and easy road section bringing you to the railway station right next to the impressive Citadel marking the entrance to the city. Well done Carlisle!

CARLISLE

The cycle route leads to the impressive Citadel, right next to Carlisle railway station

The 'Border City' was established by the Romans to serve forts on Hadrian's Wall. Carlisle Priory was founded by King Henry I in 1122 and 10 years later became the red sandstone cathedral. Much of this building was destroyed by the Scots in the 17th century and it was restored in 1853–7. The Prior's Tower and Deanery can also be visited within the cathedral grounds, where the Prior's Kitchen serves teas, coffees and lunches.

Carlisle Castle (English Heritage) is a great medieval fortress that has watched over Carlisle for over nine centuries. It is also home to the Border Regiment Museum.

Carlisle Citadel Station was built in 1847 at the northern end of the Settle–Carlisle railway, whose steam trains still puff smoke down the line. The two towers of the Citadel were built in the 19th century, on the site of the original southern entrance to the city, for use as assize courts and a forbidding prison. The Citadel's West Tower is now open to the public for visits.

Guided town trails in Carlisle are available at the Tourist Centre in the old Town Hall.

Problem with your bike? North Pennine Cycles is in Nenthead at 'the heart of the C2C'

APPENDIX A
ROUTE SUMMARY TABLE

STAGE	START/FINISH	DISTANCE (KM/MILES)	ASCENT (M)	DESCENT (M)	TIME	PAGE
Stage 1a	Whitehaven to Keswick	50/31	863	786	3–5hrs	50
Link route	St Bees to the C2C	4/2½	120	56	20mins	64
Stage 1b	Workington to Keswick	39/24	613	533	3–5hrs	66
Link route	Whitehaven to Workington	14.5/9	152	144	1hr 15mins	73
Stage 2	Keswick to Langwathby	46/28½	597	578	4–5hrs	74
Stage 3	Langwathby to Nenthead	35/21½	977	631	4–5hrs	83
Stage 4	Nenthead to Consett	48/30	804	991	3–4hrs	92
Stage 5a	Consett to Sunderland	40/25	253	504	2–3hrs	104
Stage 5b	Consett to Tynemouth	43/27	353	577	3–5hrs	113

APPENDIX B
SUGGESTED ITINERARIES (4, 3 AND 2 DAYS)

Looking west from near the top of the off-road climb to Hartside, with the road crossing marked by a conspicuous white building

C2C IN 4 DAYS

Day 1: Whitehaven or Workington to Mungrisdale

63km (39 miles) from Whitehaven or 51km (32 miles) from Workington

5–7hrs

There is only limited time to explore Keswick and no opportunity to take the Old Coach Road. The ride from Keswick to Mungrisdale is fairly easy, starting flat and ending with gentle ups and downs. Mungrisdale is in a superb position at the eastern end of the Lakeland fells. There are wonderful walks on the doorstep – you may wish to stay an extra night to explore.

Day 2: Mungrisdale to Garrigill or Alston

60km (37 miles) or 58km (36 miles)

5–7hrs

A low-level ride to Penrith, followed by undulating country with views of the Pennine chain ahead. The route culminates in the long climb up Hartside, after which it's all downhill towards the village of Garrigill or nearby Alston.

Day 3: Garrigill or Alston to Parkhead

39km (24 miles) or 44km (27 miles)

4–5hrs

A comparatively short distance, with plenty of climbs and a long off-road ride across Stanhope Common that slows things down. Do not make the mistake of assuming it's all downhill after reaching the highest point of the C2C at Black Hill. There is plenty more climbing to be done, and it is a pleasure to reach old Parkhead Station, after which it really is downhill.

The self-service Cyclists' Barn, right next to the Greystoke Cycle Café, provides a warm welcome to all cyclists who arrive on their bikes

Day 4: Parkhead to Tynemouth or Sunderland

60km (37 miles) or 55km (34 miles)

4–5hrs or 3–5hrs

Exactly the same as on the five-day itinerary. Do not underestimate the time required to get to the finish.

C2C IN 3 DAYS

Day 1: Whitehaven or Workington to Greystoke

76km (47 miles) or 64km (40 miles)

7–8hrs+

A tough first day that will appeal to enthusiastic cyclists who are fit. Greystoke, best known for the legend of Tarzan, is a pleasant village on the C2C route and a pleasant place to stay. Alternatively, ride another 9.5km (6 miles) to Penrith to finish the day.

Day 2: Greystoke to Allenheads

66km (41 miles)

7–8hrs+

The village of Allenheads is a fine place to rest at the end of a very tough day, with strength-sapping climbs up Hartside, out of Garrigill and up Black Hill as the route tackles the biggest hills of the C2C.

Day 3: Allenheads to Tynemouth or Sunderland

80km (50 miles) or 76km (47 miles)

6–8hrs+

There is still some tough cycling to be done, with a stiff climb out of Allenheads and slow progress on the off-road route across Stanhope Common. After that it's pretty much all downhill to the end of the C2C.

Stopping for a break by a drystone wall in fine surroundings on the road to Garrigill

C2C IN 2 DAYS

Day 1: Whitehaven or Workington to Garrigill	Day 2: Garrigill to Tynemouth or Sunderland
124km (77 miles) or 113km (70 miles)	98km (61 miles) or 93km (58 miles)
10hrs+	7–9hrs+

This is a very long section, which culminates in tackling half of the big climbs across the Pennines. It is difficult to make this section shorter because there are so few places to stay between Langwathby, almost 32km (20 miles) back along the route, and Garrigill. If you want to ride the C2C in two days, there is a price!

Another long day, with tough climbs out of Garrigill and Allenheads followed by a long off-road section across Stanhope Moor, unless you opt for a faster ride on the road. After this, the downhill ride from Parkhead to Tynemouth or Sunderland will probably seem like a long way to the end.

APPENDIX C
USEFUL CONTACTS

Sustrans information

www.sustrans.org.uk
A mine of information on UK National Cycle Network routes. There's also a dedicated Sustrans C2C page with a link through to the Sustrans shop if you wish to buy the official C2C map. Check for important route updates, such as temporary route closures, new link routes or variants.

CTC (Cycle Touring Club)

www.ctc.org.uk
The UK's national cyclists' organisation offers advice and services for all types of cycling.

Bag-carrying services

Sherpa:
www.sherpavan.com

The Bicycle Transport Co:
Tel: 01207 240400

Stanley Travel:
www.bikebus.uk.com

Cycle Transport North East:
www.newcastlecitytours.co.uk/cycletrans.php

C2C tour operators

Mickledore Travel:
www.mickledore.co.uk

Saddle Skedaddle:
www.skedaddle.co.uk/search/C2C

Cycle Active:
www.cycleactive.com

Adventure Cycling:
www.adventurecycling.co.uk

Xplore Britain Cycling:
www.xplorebritain.com

C2C Hassle Free:
www.c2chasslefree.co.uk

Trailbrakes (C2C package):
www.trailbrakes.co.uk/output/home.asp

Tourist information centres
Whitehaven
Market Hall, Market Place CA28 7JG
Tel: 01946 852939;
email: tic@copelandbc.gov.uk

Workington
Carnegie Theatre, Finkle Street CA14 3BD
Tel: 01900 606699;
email: workingtontic@allerdale.gov.uk

Cockermouth
Town Hall, Market Street CA13 9NP
Tel: 01900 822634;
email: cockermouthtic@co-net.com

Keswick
Moot Hall, Market Square CA12 5JR
Tel: 01768 77645;
email: Keswicktic@lake-district.gov.uk

Penrith
Penrith Museum, Middlegate CA11 7PT
Tel: 01768 867466;
email: pen.tic@eden.gov.uk

Carlisle
The Old Town Hall CA3 8JE
Tel: 01228 625600;
email: Tourism@Carlisle-City.gov.uk

Alston
Town Hall, Front Street CA9 3RF
Tel: 01434 382244;
email: Alston.tic@eden.gov.uk

Beamish
North of England Open Air Museum
DH9 0RG
Tel: 0191 370 4000

Stanhope
Durham Dales Centre, Castle Gardens,
Weardale DL13 2FJ
Tel: 01388 527650;
email: durham.dales.centre@
durham.gov.uk

Newcastle
Central Exchange Buildings,
132 Grainger Street NE1 5AF
Tel: 0191 277 8000;
email: tourist.info@newcastle.gov.uk

North Shields
Unit 18, Royal Quays NE29 6DW
Tel: 0191 2005895

Sunderland
50 Fawcett Street SR1 1RF
Tel: 0191 5532001/2;
email: tourist.info@sunderland.gov.uk

Accommodation websites

www.dalesandvales.co.uk
Excellent accommodation website covering much of the C2C route.

www.c2c-guide.co.uk
The C2C website provides comprehensive information on where to sleep, eat and drink, using a drop-down menu for towns, villages and sections of the route from west to east.

www.c2cplaces2stay.co.uk
This site is run by a team of web designers based in Penrith who are keen cyclists. It shows where to stay, eat, drink, shop, fix your bike and other useful things.

www.bedsforcyclists.co.uk
Beds for Cyclists is a very user-friendly website made by cyclists for cyclists that maps cycle-friendly accommodation against the National Cycle Network, including long-distance routes. Go to www.bedsforcyclists.co.uk/routes/Coast_to_Coast_Route_Map.php for the C2C route.

Bike-hire companies

Haven Cycles C2C Services:
www.havencycles-c2cservices.co.uk

Pedal Power:
www.pedal-power.co.uk

Ainfield Cycles:
www.pedal-power.co.uk

Darke Cycles:
www.peterdarkecycles.com

Cycle Transport North East:
www.newcastlecitytours.co.uk/cycletrans.php

APPENDIX D
RIDING THE C2C FROM EAST TO WEST

Whether you ride the C2C from west to east or east to west, there are good hills, bad hills, great views, enjoyable parts of the route and less enjoyable parts of the route. Although it is commonly held that the hills are tougher from east to west – all in all, things end up pretty even after 225km (140 miles) in either direction. Obviously, prevailing winds blowing in from the Atlantic do not help when you are riding towards the west. If gales are forecast, the struggle factor increases, and it's no fun riding head-first into driving rain (but, equally, cyclists going the other way could also be unlucky and find themselves battling against a strong easterly). In this direction, the route stars either at Sunderland or Tynemouth.

Option A: Sunderland (Roker) to Consett
The route requires a lot more pedalling in a westerly direction, with a gradual climb towards Consett, but is generally undemanding and well protected from prevailing winds.

Option B: Tynemouth to Consett
This is a steady climb on an easy gradient, with the Derwent Walk cycle path well protected from prevailing winds.

Consett to Rookhope
The uphill gradient is a little steeper on the Waskerley Way from Consett to Parkhead, but still undemanding, unless you are riding against strong westerlies, as much of this cycle path

A local mountain biker enjoys a superb descent, heading west from Bolts Law

is very exposed to the prevailing wind direction.

Cyclists opting for the off-road route across the grouse moors to the west of Parkhead are advised to follow the road through to Edmonbyers Common before turning onto the bridleway, thus missing out the first narrow section of track, which can be muddy and difficult to ride in either direction. From the top at Bolts Law, there are superb views ahead across the Pennines, with a great downhill all the way to Rookhope. The road route goes steeply downhill on the B6278 to Stanhope, then follows a lane up and down to Rookhope.

Rookhope to Nenthead

Unfortunately, there's a big climb past the Lintzgarth Arch and Grove Rake Mine from about 330m to 533m above sea level. This is the best downhill of the C2C going east, but the uphill gradient is fairly steady going west, and there is plenty of time to admire the wonderful views.

The C2C winds steeply downhill into Allenheads, but then gets tough with another 200m of vertical climbing on a steady uphill to 569m on Shivery Hill – aptly named if you're unfortunate enough to get soaked while trying to ride against a westerly gale, as this is very open country.

Enjoy a relaxing freewheel downhill in preparation for another steady uphill to 609m close to Black Hill, rated by Sustrans as the highest point of the C2C. From there it's downhill

all the way to Nenthead on the off-road route, which is recommended for fabulous views to the west in fine weather, or there is a more undulating route on the longer tarmac road.

Nenthead to Hartside Top

There is a seriously steep climb out of Nenthead heading west up Dowgang Hush to 599m, which must be the steepest road on the entire C2C. A ride to the top is very, very tough.

Once at the top, just below the brow of Nunner Hill, it's down, down, down, with a magnificent descent to Garrigill and fabulous views (it is rather pleasing to think that this series of hills can feel pretty ghastly for those riding in the opposite direction). Watch out for the junction with the B6277 – if there's any traffic, you have to stop and give way. Also watch out for the final descent to Low Houses Bridge, where the gradient gets extremely steep, so be prepared to pull on your brakes.

(For anyone wishing to divert to the nearby market town of Alston, it's an easy ride to the north from Garrigill, via the relatively quiet B6277. Rejoin the C2C route via Route 68 to Leadgate, following the other side of the River South Tyne valley.)

From Garrigill, follow Route 7 on an easy lane to Leadgate, then turn left for a stiff uphill to join the A686. Unfortunately, there is no way of getting to Hartside Top Café at 580m apart from grinding uphill on the main road. It's a steady gradient and the views are nice, but 6.5km (4 miles) is a long way, particularly on a busy weekend with cars and motorbikes blasting past your slothful bike. Riding up here in bad westerly weather could be dreadful.

Hartside Top to Penrith

You will be relieved to reach Hartside Top! From here, there are two options. First is the off-road route downhill. It is the most peaceful option, with superb views across to the Lakeland fells ahead, but the first part is steep and difficult enough to be a 'technical' descent on a mountain bike. The second option, the road route, is recommended for hybrids or touring bikes. Follow the A686 for just over 1.5km (1 mile) as it wiggles downhill, also providing fine views, and keep your hands on the brakes in order not to miss the C2C right turn, which

comes up just after some quarries on a 90° bend. Remember that this is an A-road, and take great care crossing. If you have any doubts, pull into the side and walk your bike across the A686 to join the lane that slaloms downhill to Selah Bridge, where it joins the alternative off-road section.

From Selah Bridge, the westbound C2C provides a superb downhill to Renwick, with the option of a rough off-road downhill for mountain bikers. Route 7 heads south through peaceful countryside towards Langwathby, with regular ups and downs including a few short, sharp climbs, but nothing dramatic. Take time to visit Long Meg and Her Daughters (stone circle) before riding on to Langwathby.

Cross the River Eden on Langwathby Bridge, following Route 7 on a pleasant lane that climbs steadily towards the Beacon Plantation on

Having crossed the high barrier of the Pennines, the C2C follows quiet up-and-down lanes westwards towards the Lake District, with the next big climbs beyond Keswick

The Old Coach Road provides a wonderful off-road alternative on the C2C, heading towards Keswick

the high hillside above Penrith, where you can enjoy fine views to the south before plunging steeply downhill into the centre of the town.

Penrith to Keswick and Thornthwaite

Follow Route 7 under the M6 and towards Carlisle, turning west towards Greystoke on Route 71 with its steady, undemanding ups-and-downs. You may like to try following the Old Coach Road route to Keswick (see 'Taster routes', Route 4), which works best in a westerly direction. The road route is reasonably undemanding and provides superb views of Bowscale and Carrock Fell at the eastern end of the Lake District National Park, particularly when taking the alternative

'quiet' route via Mungrisdale, which is highly recommended.

The main route follows the direction of the A66 westwards past Threlkeld before joining the railway path that zooms cyclists into the centre of Keswick, with a negligible gradient and good protection against westerly weather systems.

From Keswick, follow Route 71 on an easy road route to Braithwaite, then join a quiet lane (parallel to the raucous A66) heading towards the south-west corner of Bassenthwaite. Here there is a three-way sign for the C2C, offering alternative finish points at Whitehaven or Workington.

Option A: Thornthwaite to Whitehaven

It's a long, steady uphill climb through Whinlatter Forest on forestry tracks, but mellow enough for cyclists to keep pushing the pedals most of the way, with excellent protection from westerlies. Cross the road a short way downhill from the visitor centre, then continue westwards on forestry tracks, with fairly gentle ups and downs on the crossing of Whinlatter Pass before the start of a superb downhill on a narrow lane to Lorton Vale, with wonderful views towards the west coast and Solway Firth.

From High Lorton, the C2C route has been diverted to the east side of the River Cocker since Lorton Bridge was washed away and it crosses the river by Scale Hill en route to Loweswater, mainly following narrow lanes with fairly gentle ups and downs.

Past Loweswater is the start of a long and steady climb towards Lamplugh, with the landscape opening out, which is great for views but not so great in strong westerly headwinds. A series of swooping ups and downs leads through the village of Kirkland, with only a short distance to climb to the top of the final hill.

From there, it's a steady downhill gradient all the way to the west coast, following the traffic-free cycle path through to the outskirts of Whitehaven, followed by a final

Looking west, a superb downhill from Whinlatter Pass to High Lorton with wonderful views towards the Irish Sea and Solway Firth

C2C start or finish at Workington

signposted ride through the fringes of the town to the finish at the harbour.

Option B: Thornthwaite to Workington

The climb up through Wythop Woods on this route is more varied and dramatic than the Whitehaven route, with a very steep final section to ride out of the woods. One advantage of this route is that it's almost all downhill from this point, as the general trend is flat, with the route following the side of the River Derwent valley through to Workington. There are some ups and downs on the way to Cockermouth, but nothing steep or challenging, with an excellent cycle-friendly route through the town.

A few more ups and downs need to be negotiated riding westwards out of Cockermouth, including an unexpectedly steep climb through Great Broughton and a final climb through Camerton, where the route joins a tarmac cycle path that leads to the River Derwent on the outskirts of Workington. Here, turn upstream to cross the river on a footpath/cycle bridge, following C2C signposts past the railway station to ride along the south side of the docks, heading for the remote lighthouse that signals the end of the C2C.

APPENDIX E

PRE-RIDE BIKE MEDICAL

Giving your bike a thorough pre-ride medical will guarantee you a much more comfortable ride and probably save a lot of roadside fiddling.

- **Drive train** Check chain rings, sprockets and chain for wear. Make sure the chain is clean and well lubricated, and has not stretched.

- **Wheels** Check rims are not bent and spokes are taut. Also check for wear on the side walls. Make sure the quick-release skewers that lock the wheels to the frame can be locked and unlocked. Listen to the bearings when the wheels are spun. Nasty noises may mean rusty bearings seizing up inside.

- **Tyres** Check tread is in good condition, there are no cuts, and tyres are blown hard, with virtually no 'give' when you push in the sides, indicating optimum pressure.

- **Headset** Check that the bearings inside the head tube, which allow the handlebars to turn, are smooth. Any stiffness or grinding probably indicates lack of lubrication.

- **Front forks** Check the front forks don't move back when the front brake is applied.

- **Handlebars** Check the handlebars are at right angles to the forks, with allen-key bolts screwed tight.

- **Bottom bracket** Check that cranks cannot move from side to side. Listen to your bottom bracket bearings.

- **Pedals** Check that each pedal is screwed tightly to each crank. Remember that the right pedal has a conventional clockwise thread, while the left pedal has an unconventional anti-clockwise thread. Listen to your pedal bearings.

- **Brakes** Check that they work! Your brakes will get a huge amount of use on the C2C and must be fail-safe. On bikes with conventional brakes, such as V-brakes, check the pads for wear, replace if necessary and make sure they are correctly aligned on the rims with the allen bolts done up tight. Check that the brake cables move easily. If they don't, consider replacing both inner wires and outer covers. On bikes with disc brakes, check that they are functioning perfectly. If there is any problem with hydraulic fluid or disc pads, get a bike mechanic to do the work unless you are totally confident.

- **Suspension** Check that suspension bounces up and down, with no nasty noises. Read the manual and use a grease gun to lubricate forks as instructed. Use a suspension pump to increase pressure as instructed. Unless you are very keen on DIY mechanics, servicing front or rear suspension is best performed by a professional mechanic.

- **Gears** Check the gear cables move easily and are exactly the correct length for a smooth change to every gear. Use the front and rear derailleur to move up and down the chain rings and sprockets, ensuring that the chain engages cleanly every time. If the cable has stretched, use the barrel adjuster to shorten the length until changes are perfect. If the cable sticks inside the housing, replace with a new cable and consider a new housing.

- **Saddle** Check that your saddle is comfortable. If not, buying a new one will probably give a psychological boost. The saddle should be high enough for your leg to be virtually straight on the downstroke. The fore-and-aft position of the saddle is also important. Your backside should rest on the wide point with a relaxed reach to the handlebars. Use an allen key to slide the saddle a few millimetres forwards or backwards on its rails, until it feels just right. At the same time adjust the horizontal angle of the saddle, which should be parallel to the top tube of the bike or slightly angled, with the nose higher than the seat.

- **Mudguards** Check that mudguards are securely attached to the frame, with all nuts tight and no part rubbing against the wheels.

- **Racks** Check that racks are securely attached to the frame, with all nuts tight. Do not exceed the maximum load.

- **Lights** Put in new batteries and check functionality.

APPENDIX F

MENDING A PUNCTURE

Punctures are one of those things about cycling – a common hazard like wasp stings!

- If the bike starts to feel funny – normally a bit wobbly and irresponsive – stop and push each tyre with your thumb to check pressure. A squidgy tyre indicates that you have a puncture. An audible hiss indicates a big puncture.

- Do not ride the bike with a flat or even partly flat tyre. It's not at all pleasant and risks damaging the tube, tyre and rim.

- Push the bike to a pleasant, quiet place where you can mend the puncture, well away from passing traffic.

- Take out your tool kit and turn the bike upside-down.

- Unlock the quick-release and unscrew the skewer a few turns anti-clockwise, until it is possible to lift the wheel out of the 'drop-outs' at the base of the forks or frame. If your bike has conventional brakes with wire cables, the straddle wire will probably need undoing. If your bike has hydraulic disc brakes, do not pull on the brake handle with

the wheel out, as this will jam the discs closed.

- Lay the wheel down on the ground and make sure it is fully deflated – undo the little brass screw and push in (narrow Presta valve) or push in the pin (wide Schraeder valve).

- Work the angled end of a tyre lever under the edge of the tyre. Flip the lever back through 180° and lock the end under a spoke to hold it in position. You can then work a second tyre lever under the tyre. Unless the tyre is very tight, this will be enough to get the tyre off one side of the rim. Simply pull the lever round in a sweeping circle.

- Undo the screw fitting that holds the valve onto the rim. Put it in a safe place with the end cap – do not just drop them in the grass.

- Take out the tube and inflate with the pump. If it doesn't blow up at all, you probably have an irreparable puncture caused by a big cut or the valve breaking away from the tube. The solution is to put in a new inner tube. If the tube does inflate, listen for the hiss of escaping air. You may need to put your ear right next to the rubber when there is a small hole. If you can hear nothing, try putting the tube under water and look for bubbles.

- When the puncture is located, it's time to put on a patch. Make sure the area is dry. Roughen it with sandpaper. Apply a thin layer of glue over the immediate area. Wait for at least 5mins until it is almost dry – if you don't wait, the patch may not stick properly. During this time, run your fingers round the inside of the tyre. If anything sharp is poking through, it will need to be removed.

- Peel off the silver backing paper and apply the patch, pushing down the feather edges. The tyre should be lightly inflated for a good fit when you push it back under the tyre and onto the rim.

- Be very careful pushing the edge of the tyre back onto the rim. Start opposite the valve and work around in two semi-circles with your hands.

For the final push, a tyre lever is normally needed to get the whole tyre back onto the rim. Be careful not to catch and tear the inner tube. Make sure the inner tube is completely inside the tyre, with no part trapped against the edge of the rim.

- Push the wheel back into the drop-outs. Tighten the skewer with a few clockwise turns and close the quick release.

- Tighten the screw fitting that holds the valve onto the rim, making sure the valve sticks out at 90°. Use the pump to blow up the tyre as hard as possible, then screw tight the valve (Presta) and screw on the outer cap.

- Turn the bike the right way up. If you have cable brakes, remember to re-attach the straddle wire before you ride the bike.

- Pick up all the bits, pack away your tool kit and continue the C2C!

NOTES

NOTES

NOTES

LISTING OF CICERONE GUIDES

For full information on all our
guides, and to order books and
eBooks, visit our website:
www.cicerone.co.uk.

Walking – Trekking – Mountaineering – Climbing – Cycling

Over 40 years, Cicerone have built up an outstanding collection of 300 guides, inspiring all sorts of amazing adventures.

Every guide comes from extensive exploration and research by our expert authors, all with a passion for their subjects. They are frequently praised, endorsed and used by clubs, instructors and outdoor organisations.

All our titles can now be bought as **e-books** and many as iPad and Kindle files and we will continue to make all our guides available for these and many other devices.

Our website shows any **new information** we've received since a book was published. Please do let us know if you find anything has changed, so that we can pass on the latest details. On our **website** you'll also find some great ideas and lots of information, including sample chapters, contents lists, reviews, articles and a photo gallery.

It's easy to keep in touch with what's going on at Cicerone, by getting our monthly **free e-newsletter**, which is full of offers, competitions, up-to-date information and topical articles. You can subscribe on our home page and also follow us on **Facebook** and **Twitter**, as well as our **blog**.

Cicerone – the very best guides for exploring the world.

CICERONE

2 Police Square Milnthorpe Cumbria LA7 7PY
Tel: 015395 62069 info@cicerone.co.uk
www.cicerone.co.uk